My Life in His Paws

My Life in His Paws

The story of Ted
and how he saved me

WENDY HILLING

CORONET

First published in Great Britain in 2016 by Coronet
An imprint of Hodder & Stoughton
An Hachette UK company

First published in paperback in 2017

1

A CIP catalogue record for this title is available from the British Library.

Paperback ISBN: 978 1 473 63570 8
Ebook ISBN: 978 1 473 63568 5

Typeset in Cochin by Hewer Text UK Ltd, Edinburgh
Printed and bound by CPI Group (UK) Ltd, Croydon, CR0 4YY

Hodder & Stoughton policy is to use papers that are natural, renewable
and recyclable products and made from wood grown in sustainable
forests. The logging and manufacturing processes are expected to
conform to the environmental regulations of the country of origin.

Hodder & Stoughton Ltd
Carmelite House
50 Victoria Embankment
London EC4Y 0DZ

www.hodder.co.uk

Dedicated to all my family and friends,
especially my sister Mary, who always read
'just one more chapter' to me when we were children

Contents

Introduction

I wake up and I can't breathe or move. My throat is contracting and I can't shout for help. My husband is lying next to me and my dog, Ted, lies at the foot of the bed. They are both asleep and I can't move to wake them. I'm scared witless. They say your life flashes before your eyes when you're about to die, and it's true. I know this is desperate. I don't have much time left.

In an instant, Ted is on his feet. He rushes over to the panic button on our bedroom wall and presses it with his nose. When the operator answers, Ted is barking so she knows he's there. She expects him now: 'Hello Ted, tell Mummy and Daddy there's an ambulance on its way.' He rushes round to Peter's side of the bed and pulls at his pillow and barks to make sure he's awake. Peter turns me on my side and, after a time, I can breathe again. The relief is intense.

By the time the ambulance arrives, I'm breathing normally and starting to recover, but we are both shocked. One of the paramedics tests my oxygen levels.

'It's a good thing your husband called us so quickly,' he says. 'Even if he can get you breathing again, we need to check there hasn't been lasting damage. Seconds count when you can't breathe.'

'Oh, it wasn't my husband who called you,' I say. 'It was the dog!'

They turn to look at Ted, who is sitting on the bedroom floor, watching me to make sure I'm OK and hoping that these men will go away so he can get his well-earned treat. They can't believe it. But by now I'm used to people being amazed by Ted.

'You mean your dog just saved your life?'

'Oh yes,' I say, 'he does it all the time.' I reach down and stroke Ted's head. 'I couldn't live without him. Ted's been the making of me.'

Ted is a handsome nine-year-old golden retriever, with a beautiful pale gold coat. Like all golden retrievers, he's good-natured and eager to please, but he has a cheeky side too: he loves playing and larking about and helping himself to things he's not supposed to. But Ted is not an ordinary dog. He's my full-time carer, trained by the charity Canine Partners to care for me since he was eighteen months old. He's been by my side since he was a ten-week-old puppy. He's with me twenty-four hours a day – he helps with daily tasks, and if my life is in danger he raises the alarm. He even receives payments from the government towards his keep, in recognition of everything he does.

I was born a 'butterfly child' – my skin is as fragile as a butterfly's wing. I have a rare genetic condition called recessive dystrophic epidermolysis bullosa (EB), which means the skin is extremely delicate and even the slightest knock can cause it to tear or blister. It means every movement is difficult and causes pain. It affects the body inside and out, so the skin in my throat and mouth is very delicate too – coughing, crying or choking can all cause blistering. After years of damage, my throat is now very small and I can stop breathing at any time. I've needed full-time care for over two decades now – and Ted has been responsible for most of it for nearly eight years.

When it's time to get up, Ted uses his mouth to bring me the clothes I've laid out the night before and helps me put them on. I go to the bathroom and get in the shower. As soon as he hears the shower switch off, he brings me my towel from the radiator – unless he's decided he wants to play a game, and then he dances about with it first. 'Come on, Teddy, can I have the towel, please? I'm freezing!'

Hang on a minute, just playing!

When I'm downstairs, I say, 'Right, Teddy, are you ready to go out?'

Yes!

He fetches my shoes and his lead, which I clip on. 'Thank you. In my hand, please, Teddy,' I say, and he hands me his lead with his mouth. If the lead is caught behind his front paw, I say, 'Fix that, please,' and he steps over it. Someone once laughed at me for saying please and thank you to my dog, but I'm always polite to Teddy – he's working for me after all. I've always treated my animals with the utmost respect.

He knows where to go from my voice. 'Cup of tea, Teddy?' I'll say, and he'll take me straight to the nearest café. He knows exactly where he's going – I'd happily follow him with my eyes closed.

Ted stays on my right, to balance me – my right hip is very bad and if I fall, I fall to the right. He leads me round any holes or anything sticking up in the pavement that might cause me pain. I feel utterly safe with him – if anything happens to me, I know he'll bark and get help.

It's impossible to describe how different it is being looked after by a dog. I hate being cared for by a human now – I'm too independent. I just want to do it myself. Before Ted, my husband Peter would have to look after me when we were out, and it felt like he stopped being my husband and became my carer. It was awkward for both of us.

I used to feel self-conscious when I left the house; I knew that when people looked at me they saw only a disabled woman. But with Teddy it's a whole different story. People love him. They love to watch him do things for me. When we're out together I become invisible, but I don't mind that – I'm proud of him and the way he takes care of me. He makes me braver – if I go into a hospital for a procedure, I don't think about what they're doing to me, I'm thinking about Ted and how he is. I don't cry out or make a fuss because I don't want to upset him.

We go to the supermarket and I point at what I need. 'Can you get that for me, Teddy?' *Which one?* He looks round the shelves, moving his head up and down. 'No, not that! That one! That's it!' *Oh, that one!* He grabs it with his mouth and puts it in my basket. When we've finished, I let him take the last item to the checkout in his mouth – he likes to carry one thing himself. I have my purse in the basket and he takes it out, puts his paws up on the counter and gives it to the checkout girl. She takes the money, puts the change back and hands it back to Ted, who drops it in the basket. I think she enjoys it as much as he does. One of the great joys of having Teddy is the pleasure he gives other people, as well as the family.

Back at home, he unzips my jacket and pulls at the sleeves to help me take it off. He undoes the Velcro on my shoes and pulls them off my feet and then he pulls his Canine Partners jacket off over his head.

Ted works hard and concentrates all day, but when his jacket comes off, that's when the party begins. It's time to be silly. He always has time to relax, to play, and just be a dog. When Peter and I are out with him, people will say, 'Oh, you've got such a quiet dog!' We look at each other and start laughing – they should see him when he's at home or tearing around on the beach.

Ted rolls around on the floor on his back, chewing a squeaky toy. I grab the other end and pretend I'm trying to take it away from him – he loves playing tug with me. 'Give it to me, Teddy, it's mine!' I say. He holds on tight. But if I really need him to give it to me, I just say, 'In my hand, Teddy,' and he'll do it immediately. He knows when we're playing and when I'm serious. We know each other inside out by now.

If I need anything in the house, I can just ask Teddy to fetch it for me. If I drop anything, he picks it up for me straight away and puts it back in my hand. My hands aren't very mobile after all the scarring over the years, but no matter how many times I drop something, he'll keep picking it up for me. He doesn't give up.

The washing machine finishes its cycle. When Teddy hears the click, he starts running towards it. If Peter, my husband, gets there first, he pushes him out of the way with his shoulder – *Shove over, shove over, I'm doing it!* He knows, if he does the washing he gets a treat. He pulls the washing out of the machine, puts it in the basket and drags the basket out to the line. I sit at the washing line and he hands me each piece of clothing with his mouth, and then a peg. Although sometimes he'll make me wait, while he runs round the garden with the peg in his mouth. 'Come on, Ted!' I say. *Just playing, Mum!*

Looking after a dog means you're totally needed. It's an amazing feeling. It makes you keep going, gets you up in the morning and gives you a purpose. For years, I've been the one being cared for and now I'm caring for him. It gives me some kind of standing, in my head if nowhere else.

Ted does so much for me, but the most important thing he's given me is his friendship. If the pain gets bad, we just have a cuddle or a game. *Come on, Mum, don't think about it! Let's play instead!* Ted doesn't know I'm disabled: he just knows I'm his mum and I love him. Nothing else seems that important if I have that moment at the end of the day when I put my arms round him and snuggle into him. I think, *I can cope because I've got you*. He makes me feel weightless, like I can do anything. I can do anything if I've got Ted.

At bedtime, we give him a Bonio and that's when he knows it's time to sleep. Teddy always sleeps by my bed. Before Ted, Peter and I could sleep for only two hours at a time because someone had to be monitoring me while I slept. It was exhausting for both of us. Now, if I stop breathing, I know Ted will sense it and we rely on him to press the emergency button. We can both sleep easily now, knowing Ted's there.

He's just so much fun to be around; I'm high as a kite when we go out together. It's hard to stay confident when you have a disability – people do treat you differently and I've gone through periods of feeling really quite low and anxious. But Ted's given me a life I could only dream of. This is the story of how we found each other, through fate, hard work and two very special rescue dogs. It's a story of love, hope and determination. This is the story of me and Ted.

chapter 1

An Adventurous Child in a Delicate Body

I was born with skin not made for this world. The first sign that something was wrong came when the midwife knocked my hand and the skin came off. Soon it became clear that my skin was blistering and tearing at the slightest knock. Picking me up or trying to feed or dress me caused nasty wounds, which were very painful and often became infected. A nurse tried to turn me in my cot and all the skin came off where she'd touched me. It frightened her to death and I still had the handprint-shaped scar on the side of my body when I was in my twenties. Not long after that early experience, I was diagnosed with EB.

EB is a rare and painful condition. A faulty gene, for coding collagen VII, means that the skin isn't properly anchored to the layers underneath, so it tears and blisters very easily, both inside and outside the body. Many children with EB die in infancy and my parents were told I was unlikely to survive for more than a few days. I was christened at three days old.

To try to protect my skin I was kept in a cotton-wool crib; which has led to 'butterfly children' also being known as 'cotton wool babies'. I hated the feel of the cotton wool; it set my teeth on edge. I still hate it today.

EB is inherited, but that was never properly explained to us, and my mother was convinced that I'd caught it from the midwife who, by strange coincidence, had a son with EB. I grew up thinking that I was contagious, and whenever anyone had a baby I made sure I stayed out of the way. I didn't explain why I was doing it and put up with people thinking I was being a bit funny. My two older sisters were born with ordinary skin, but my little brother, who was born when I was sixteen, also has EB. I can still remember the day he was born: I was convinced he had caught it from me. I felt very guilty.

My childhood was spent being taken from hospital to hospital. Because EB is so rare, I used to be taken to medical conferences as a sort of exhibit. I dreaded it. Once, when I was about six, I was made to go up on stage in front of a group of medical professionals, and a doctor rubbed the skin on my hand to see how much pressure it took to blister it. He rubbed my thumb until a blister appeared. I was terrified of seeing doctors after that.

The only exception was my local doctor, who I went to see from the age of five to seventeen. He had two Airedale dogs who sat on either side of his desk, like bookends. I was allowed to stroke them: I can still remember the softness of the fur in my hands. Mum said to him, 'The only reason she comes to see you is because of those dogs!' That was the only appointment I looked forward to.

All my life, I've been given deadlines. After surviving the first few days, my parents were told that I would die when I was three. Then we were told I would probably not live beyond the age of ten. When I was old enough to understand, I was terrified. I used to try to imagine what death would be like. I was petrified when my tenth birthday came round. When I didn't die on my birthday, I thought they must have meant that I would die when I *was* ten, before I was eleven, so I spent another year frightened witless. I never told my parents about it. I knew how much it upset them, knowing that I was going to die.

Extraordinarily, there were three babies born with EB in our village – doctors now can't believe it when I tell them. One of them, a little boy, died when he was eighteen months old. I used to walk over to his grave and talk to him. I'm not sure why; I just felt so sorry for him. No matter how ill he was, he couldn't have wanted to die.

I spent most of my early years wrapped in bandages. You learn to manage EB as you get older: now, I move very carefully and think about every gesture. Everything is planned and precise: if I put my coat on, I have to ease the sleeve up to give it a bit more room or the fabric will bring up huge blisters. If I want to turn over in bed, I have to get out and carefully get in again in a different position. I have to rub ointment into my eyes every night, otherwise my eyelids will stick to my eyeballs and blister – it's agony. Everything has to be calibrated: if you walk too far one day, you might have to let the skin on your feet recover for days afterwards. It takes huge amounts of concentration and practice, and it's almost impossible for a child to master. When I was little my skin was constantly torn and blistered, and I walked about covered in bandages.

I attended the local primary school until one day, when I was about seven, a boy pushed me over and stood on my hands and refused to get off. I pulled my hands from under his feet and it took the skin off almost down to the bone. I can still remember the pain to this day. The boy wasn't told off, and the school said they couldn't cope with me, so my parents would have to find somewhere else for me to go.

Reluctantly, they decided to send me to boarding school. The doctor suggested that they choose one in Switzerland for the clean air. I liked the sound of it: I'd read the Heidi books and imagined myself halfway up a mountain, in a cosy chalet, surrounded by animals. I would still love to go to Switzerland one day. But Mum decided it was too far and I was sent to school in Broadstairs, Kent.

The school they chose was a school for children with asthma and eczema, and I was the only child with EB. Because most of the children had breathing problems, we were taken on long walks and had a lot of our lessons outside – the sea air was supposed to do them good. The walks were dreadful for me: my feet were constantly blistered. Some of the children with asthma would wake up in the night, struggling to breathe. I would try to help by sitting behind them and pressing their ribs to force the air out. Some nights were so bad that we were all bleary-eyed the next morning.

The school looked idyllic – a large old house, with a beautiful shrubbery, a kitchen garden, and well-kept lawns surrounded by trees – but the atmosphere was very cold. The nurses and teachers were strict and they just saw you as a patient, a charge. There was no love in the place.

I didn't like boarding school, but when I was little someone had told me that my parents had sent me away because they didn't want me at home – they didn't like changing my bandages. As a child, I had no idea that adults didn't always tell the truth and I believed what I was told. I thought that, if my parents didn't want me, I couldn't make a fuss or I'd have nowhere else to go, so I tried not to complain. I'd arrive at the start of term, go down to the basement, put my coat on the hook, my shoes in the cubby-hole, and cry until there was nothing left. But after that I'd get up and get on with the term. I made the most of the life I had. I learnt at an early age that you make your own happiness. As long as you acted happy, it was possible to feel happy.

I missed my parents dreadfully. They rang me every Sunday evening at 6 p.m. and I would always tell them I was well and happy. Then I would go to bed and talk to my toy panda, pretending I was talking to my mum and dad and telling them how I really felt. My mother wrote to me every day and my father wrote twice a week and they sent boxes of sweets to be shared out among all the pupils. I felt lucky: not many of the girls got letters, and very few ever had parcels. Each day after lunch, in all weathers but rain, we had to rest on camp beds in the playground. After our rest, we all lined up for one sweet each. While we ate our sweet, the staff in charge of us that day read out the letter my parents had sent me. I never minded sharing the sweets or the letters. I liked the fact the girls knew my family as well as I did.

My mother was a busy lady as she worked full time, but she always found time to write to me. Dad used to let a young man called Pip out of work a few minutes early to catch the post for my letters. Both Mum and Dad came to take me out every visiting day. We always seemed to get good weather. Dad called the days Sunny Wendy Visiting Days.

One visiting day, when I was about nine, my mum took me to a sweet shop for a treat. I chose two Caramac bars and took them to the till. As I handed over the money, the man started shouting at my mum. 'She shouldn't be allowed out! Nobody should take a child out with hands like that!' My hands were covered in bandages but you could probably see where the skin had torn underneath. I didn't leave the house without gloves on for another ten years. I couldn't bear anyone to look at my skin at all.

By far the worst thing about boarding school was that there were no animals. I was besotted with animals. My parents had got a Labrador puppy, Sammy, just before I went away. He was a quiet, gentle dog, and I adored him! When my parents walked him he would often pull on the lead, but when we went out together he was so comfortable with me that he just walked along beside me. I'd take him to the shops to get his tin of Chappie, but I couldn't carry it, so Sammy would carry it back in his mouth. He was my best friend.

Whenever I got home from boarding school I'd disappear with Sammy, up on the moors near our house. I always felt so safe with him. It made me laugh to watch him rolling in mud and paddling in the stream. He loved watching the tiny fish swimming about – it fascinated him.

I think part of the reason I was drawn to animals was because they were vulnerable, like me. If I saw something that wanted rescuing – snails, frogs, insects – I'd pick it up and take it into school with me. One day I found a baby bat in the shrubbery and I wanted to look after it, so I scooped it up and put it in the pocket of my pinafore. All I knew about bats was that they liked damp places, so I waited until everyone had gone to bed and, as it was getting dark, I put him in the bath with just the tiniest bit of water. I went back to bed and the next thing I knew I was being woken by a blood-curdling scream. The teacher on duty was shouting, 'Wendy, where are you? What on earth is in this bath?!' Out of sixty girls, she knew it had to be me. No one else was quite so mad about animals.

On Sundays, we'd walk to church through the village, and every week we'd go past a brick wall with a hole in the bottom. I was always at the back of the walk because I was afraid of people treading on my feet and damaging the skin. I let the others go on ahead and knelt down and looked through the hole. I saw the lovely grey legs of a pony in a stable.

Every Sunday I would get down on my hands and knees and look at the pony, and every Sunday I'd get in trouble for having a dirty dress. I don't know why I was so fascinated by the horse. Maybe it was because he was on his own, like I was.

I decided that I wanted to see what he looked like properly, on the other side of the wall. I think I was secretly hoping that I would take him away from the stable and run away from boarding school on his back.

I tried to run away and see him twice but I was caught both times. The third time I took two friends with me, Mary and another Wendy. We'd only got as far as the gate when the headmistress's car pulled in and she caught us in her headlights. The other two girls were allowed to go back to bed, but I was sent up to her office.

'You can't keep doing this, Wendy,' the headmistress said. 'If you're that upset, I'll ask your parents to come for an extra visiting day, if that will help you.'

'I'm sorry – would it help me?'

'Yes, would it make you less homesick? That's why you're running away, isn't it? To see your parents?'

'Oh no,' I said, 'I just wanted to see the horse in the village!'

I was a quiet, nervy child, and most of the time I sat still and did what I was told. But I had a mischievous side, which my dad encouraged. When I was at school, Dad sent me a parcel with a doll in it. I couldn't understand why; I didn't particularly like dolls and my father knew it. Its legs were fastened on by elastic and when I pulled at them, they came off. Inside the doll was a torch. We had to be in bed at 7 p.m., summer and winter, with no talking until 7 a.m. Dad knew that I didn't find it easy to be quiet that long, so he sent me the torch to read under the bed covers. At visiting day, Dad asked me how long it had taken me to find the torch and we all laughed.

I've always had a vivid imagination and I could think up mischief very easily. One day I had a brilliant idea: a midnight feast. What could be nicer? I told the girls in my dormitory to save their sandwiches at teatime for midnight that night. We all were pinafores with pockets, so it was easy to smuggle them past the staff.

That evening the excitement was electric. We put the sandwiches in our lockers and spent the evening whispering ghost stories. But as it got late, we got tired and fell asleep. The next minute we were being woken up for breakfast. Horrified, we tried to flush the stale, dry sandwiches down the toilets. It took ages and we were all late for breakfast.

I was an adventurous child in a delicate body. I found it very difficult to accept I could not join in the games other children played. I tried to play tennis but holding the racket caused huge black blisters on the palms of my hands. Hockey was a definite no, though when I saw how big and heavy the hockey sticks were I was quite relieved! But I hated sitting still. I still do. When the other children went out to play, I had to sit in a room by myself. I was given bottles of milk that had warmed up during the day. I can't stand the taste of warm milk now. Even the memory of it makes me feel sick.

One thing I could join in with was dance classes. It was very painful on my feet, but it was worth it. At home, my mother had taught ballroom dancing and I used to love watching her float around the dance floor in beautiful dresses, sequins glinting. The man who taught with her had a dog and I would sit with it in its basket, watching the lessons and wishing I could join in. When all the pupils had gone home, my mum's dance partner would put on some music, stand me on his feet and dance me around the floor. It was wonderful. I felt like a princess.

At school, we were taught the Margaret Morris form of dance, which encouraged free expression. I loved it. If my skin had been strong enough on my feet I would have loved to have become a dancer. I watch my sister Mary dance now and it takes me back to all those years ago.

One sunny day, we were having a dancing lesson in the common room, with the big sash windows wide open at the bottom. The most wonderful thing happened: my dog Sammy leapt through the window and rushed through the class to find me at the back of the room. At first he ignored all the other children and just cuddled me, but eventually he let everyone hug him. It was not a scheduled visiting day so I had no idea my parents were there. I buried my face in his fur and cried with happiness. I will remember that day for the rest of my life.

I always wanted to do more than I was supposed to do. I didn't mind getting hurt if it meant I could do something I really wanted. My aunt once let me hold a baby rabbit and it jumped out of my grip, taking the skin off my hands. Everyone was very shocked, but I had just been glad to hold the rabbit. I realised then that other people were more frightened of me getting hurt than I was. If I really wanted to do something, I could just weigh up the discomfort of hurting myself against the pleasure it could bring and decide if it was worth it. Once I'd worked that out, I was much happier.

One day, when I was about eight, we were taken down to the beach for lessons. Most of the lessons took place outside, to help the other children with their breathing difficulties. A kind man said that he'd like to pay for us all to have a donkey ride on the beach. I couldn't believe it! It was a dream come true. It would almost be like riding my pony.

'The others can ride the donkey, but not her,' the teacher said. 'She's got something different wrong with her and she'll get hurt.'

I was absolutely devastated. I pleaded with her to let me have a go.

'No, Wendy, you can't,' she said. 'It'll damage the skin on your legs.'

'I'll be fine! My skin's strong enough, I promise! Please, please let me have a go!'

She looked at me doubtfully. I looked back at her, pleading.

'It looks like it'll do her more harm not to have a go,' the man remarked.

The teacher sighed. 'Oh, go on then,' she said.

I did get hurt. The saddle took the skin off the inside of my legs but I didn't say anything. The air stung my raw skin as we walked back to school that afternoon.

Later I had to see matron to get my legs dressed. I was worried she'd be angry, but she just smiled and said, 'I hope the donkey was worth it!'

It was.

When I was about thirteen, my parents took me out on visiting day. We went to a beautiful park in Herne Bay. I couldn't walk very far around the grounds, so I sat with Sammy and cuddled him while my parents walked on. I told him how I hated going away from him and how I wanted to be at home, but I had to go away because I wasn't wanted by my parents.

The next thing I knew, I was in my father's arms and my mother was crying. They hadn't been far away and they'd overheard me talking to Sammy.

'Of course we love you! We thought you were so happy at boarding school!' Mum said. 'You hardly stay in when you're at home and you always seem so keen to go back after the holidays.'

'That's it, you're coming home with us now,' Dad said.

In the end, it was decided that I ought to wait till the end of the term, as it wouldn't be fair on the other girls if I just disappeared. It was the longest term ever. I wish I'd told my parents how I had felt before. I suppose I was always afraid that they'd confirm what I'd been told. It would have been unbearable to hear them say they didn't want me.

chapter 2

A Love of Animals

I'll never forget the day I first saw a golden retriever. I was seven years old and at my grandma's house – we always went to see my grandma on Sunday afternoons. Dad would fall asleep on the sofa and my sister Mary and I would do crafts together. One Sunday, the door to the living room opened and four gleaming bodies rushed in. It felt like the room had filled with sunshine.

Oh, they were beautiful! Four golden retrievers, swishing about and showing off, their coats glistening and rippling. I was absolutely entranced. Then I heard my aunty Gwen say, 'Oh, sorry, I didn't know Wendy was here!' The door shut and the beautiful golden fur disappeared.

My aunty Gwen's family bred golden retrievers. They kept four bitches and a stud dog, and they sold their litters. Aunty Gwen came to visit my grandma several times when I was there, but she was never allowed to bring the dogs near me. One day, I begged her to let me stroke them. I can still remember the feeling of that soft, golden fur in my hands. It was magical.

It was clear I adored them. Eventually, Aunty Gwen asked if I'd like to go to a dog show with them. I couldn't think of anything I'd like more. I began to go and stay with her and her husband, Uncle Fred, and it turned out they were the only people who treated me as though I had normal skin. They never fussed over me or told me to be careful. I used to love staying with them. Uncle Fred was a painter and decorator and one afternoon, he let me help him paint a window frame. Aunty Gwen told me later I was the only person besides Fred who was allowed to hold a paintbrush in their house.

The dogs never hurt me: they were bouncy but so gentle. When the dogs had had a litter, I would take the puppies out for a walk with Gwen's son, Michael. I'd go out surrounded by lots of puppies – heaven! The walking hurt my feet, but it was worth it.

I helped groom the older dogs and I went along to dog shows with them. I always made such a fuss of them – they got to know me and became fond of me. At the shows, Aunty Gwen suggested we take it in turns to stay with our dogs so that we'd all have a chance to look round. I didn't care about that; I would have happily stayed with her dogs all day. I used to have to hide when they were in the ring – I cuddled them so much that if they'd seen me, they would have made a beeline for me and not performed properly. I had to peek, though. I loved to watch the dogs show off, with their tails wagging happily.

When I was fifteen, my aunt took me and their dog Camrose Gay Delight of Sladeham to Crufts in London. It was such a wonderful day. I spent the whole time cuddling Gay when she was not in the ring. Aunty Gwen's dogs loved showing. As soon as they saw the bag she kept for dog shows with all their things in it, they got really excited. I think most golden retrievers are born show-offs. They love attention.

It was their happiness I loved. The pure happiness – they just burst with it. I've never seen a miserable golden retriever. They have such lovely natures – they always want to please. And the colour . . . that gleaming gold. I was head over heels in love

After boarding school, I started at the secondary modern. I was about fourteen and all the other girls had been there a few years already. I was still covered in bandages – I must have looked like a mummy. Only one girl was kind to me, Rose. She understood my skin and looked out for me. She would walk behind me on the busy stairways so that no one knocked me with their satchels. There was a bond between us. When we were together we felt OK. Rose was a wonderful friend to me over the years.

Luckily my life was full outside school. Although I

was passionate about golden retrievers, I was still completely and utterly in love with horses, and I wanted one of my own. There was a horse for sale in the village: he was called Valentino and he was black with a white patch on his head in the shape of a heart. I adored him and started to visit him every day. My mum had just bought a bike for my sister Mary, so I asked if she would buy me Valentino.

'No, Wendy,' she said. 'Horses need feeding. Bikes don't.'

OK then, I thought. *I'd better start saving*.

I took an old Milk Tray box, cut out a hole in the top, and Sellotaped a lid to it. That became my money box, where I kept my funds for the pony. In the meantime, I was going to learn to ride.

I went to the local riding school for lessons. I didn't tell anyone about my EB. There was a quiet horse, Robin at the stables, and I knew that if I could ride him I could get away without doing too much damage to my skin. I was still wearing gloves every day, so no one had to know how bad my hands were.

I lived for the riding lessons. I got two shillings and sixpence as pocket money but the lessons cost double that. I could just have gone every fortnight but that wasn't enough, so I worked at the stables every weekend, cleaning tacks and mucking out, to make up the difference.

One day, I arrived for the lesson and the only free horse was a very strong horse called Black Magic. They wouldn't carry over the time I'd stored up from helping

– if I didn't ride then, I'd miss my chance that week and I couldn't bear that. I didn't want allowances made for me either, so I thought I'd try Black Magic.

We got down the road and I realised I had no control whatsoever. Black Magic was pulling like anything and my hands were burning with pain. When we got to the field I panicked because I knew he would never stop for me. I did the only thing I could think of: I broke away from the ride and headed back to the stables.

I untacked Black Magic and tied him up by his stable, wondering what on earth I was going to do. I had biked there but I had no idea how to get home. By this time my hands were bleeding through my gloves.

When the instructor got back, he was furious. He couldn't believe I'd gone back alone. He told me I couldn't come back for lessons if I didn't do as I was told. I didn't know what to say. I thought about just turning round and going home, but I was so upset, knowing that they thought badly of me. So I took my gloves off and showed him why I came back. My hands, where any skin was left, were covered in black blisters. He was horrified.

'How on earth can you ride when it causes so much damage?' he asked.

'That's just it,' I said. 'I can't ride without hurting myself, but I can't not ride.'

'But why didn't you tell us?'

'I didn't want anyone to treat me differently.'

I made him promise never to tell anyone. Dad came and took me home with my bike. All he said was, 'You need to work out what you can and can't do. You're very brave, even braver than you think sometimes, but you need to be careful.'

Horses were in my blood. No amount of getting hurt would stop me.

I was sixteen and my O levels were coming up. I'd surprised everyone by doing quite well at secondary school, even though I hadn't had much teaching at boarding school, where it was their job to make sure we stayed healthy and education came second. My sister Mary had just gone to college and my mum told me, 'If you pass your exams, you can go to college like Mary.' *Oh hell!* I thought. I couldn't think of anything I wanted to do less. I couldn't bear the thought of going to another institution. All I wanted to do was to leave school and start working so I could save money for my pony. I decided I'd have to make sure I failed the exams.

My first exam came round. English Literature. I refused to write anything: I just put my pen down and sat back in my chair. Afterwards, the headmaster called me into his office and asked what on earth I thought I was doing.

'I don't want to go to college,' I said. 'I was at boarding school for seven years and I'm fed up with confined places. I want to start living. I want to work and I want my own pony.'

He sighed. 'Well, part of me doesn't blame you.'

It was taken for granted that I would never be able to work. My doctor had told me that I'd need too much time off, for hospital visits and days off when my blisters would be painful and infected. But by then I'd learnt that I didn't always have to listen when people told me what I couldn't do. After all, if everything the doctors had said had been true, I wouldn't be alive. And I wanted a pony. So I had to work.

They were advertising jobs for telephonists at the GPO and I applied without telling my mum. I got the job and went away to train. In hindsight, it was the worst thing I could have gone for because you had to wear a plastic headset. They were so heavy in those days and it took the skin off my ears. I tried attaching foam to it, but it didn't really help. It was ever so painful, but all I could think about was the pony. I was obsessed. The other girls were spending their wages on clothes and make-up, but I saved every penny. Six months later, I saw an advert for an unbroken Welsh pony.

He was forty-eight guineas and I had only forty-eight pounds. I asked my mum to loan me the rest and she agreed. But when I got him and my mother saw how wild he was, she got worried and didn't want me to ride him. She made an appointment for me to see a dermatologist in London in the hope that he would tell me to stop riding.

We all went down to London to see the doctor – me, my parents and my little brother, who was still a baby.

We all went to London Zoo together. My father got a wheelchair for me, but I refused to go in it – I was too stubborn. I walked around the zoo with my feet sore and bleeding. My mother should have known then that I was unlikely to listen to the doctor.

But when we saw him, what he said took us both by surprise. Mum had explained that I had bought a wild pony and she wanted to stop me riding it.

'Let her try,' he said. 'It's better than wrapping her up in cotton wool. She'll stop riding if she finds she gets hurt.'

He obviously didn't know me very well! My mother looked doubtful.

'A lot of people with EB are wheelchair-bound, with little hope of riding or doing any of the things Wendy wants to do,' the doctor said. 'It's good that she wants to try things. If she wants to have a go, let her.'

Looking back, I think the doctor had hit on the reason I insisted on doing things people said I couldn't. It was because I couldn't let the EB get the better of me. I needed to find my own way to deal with pain, and to me it was about not giving in, keeping alive. I felt like something was coming up behind me, and if I stopped it'd catch me.

I haven't changed. I'm still just as stubborn today. If someone tells me I can't do something, I just want to do it more.

I called my pony Frisky. They told me he was four when I got him but I found out later he was only two. He was dappled grey with a white mane and tail – my mum said he looked like a little circus pony. I broke him in, though everything had to be covered in sheep-skin – the stirrups and saddle. I biked miles to see him, come rain or shine. I lived for riding. All I ever thought of was horses.

It's difficult not to lose confidence when you have EB – people do treat you differently. Sometimes they talk to you like you can't understand them or they don't want to go near your skin. The memory of the man in the sweet shop stayed with me. It was only when I was out with animals that I felt OK, that I felt I had some standing, some right to be there. A lot of people are scared stiff of horses, but I could ride them. It was only with the horses that it felt OK to be me.

Eventually I sold Frisky on. I was always too tall to ride him, really – it was a good job I never weighed a lot! He went on to win at the White City Horse of the Year Show. When I saw him again, fifteen years later, he was pure white. I didn't know when I got him that they go white when they get older. He was a round little dumpling by then. I don't think he remembered me but I spent ages talking to him and his owners.

I had a few rescue horses who I'd take on, get them well and sell them on again to people I could trust. That's when I heard about Jack, who was for sale because he was giving his owner trouble. He would bolt at the slightest thing.

When I met him, I saw what she meant. He was lively, to say the least. He wouldn't let me ride him at first, and I couldn't get him to do anything. 'Come on, let's go through the gateway,' I'd say and he would just refuse. Gradually, I learnt not to walk in front and pull him: if I just stood to the side of him and walked him through gently, he'd go with me. He didn't like being forced into anything.

I learnt to accept that if he bolted, he bolted. And he did bolt! Once, he took off with me on his back and ran straight across the main road by his field. It was a Saturday and the road was packed with lorries going to market. I thought he was going to kill me. If you tried to turn him, he sped up and turned the other way. He leaned over on his side to turn, the way motorcyclists do. It was terrifying.

My dad gave me a suggestion: 'If he bolts, just tell him to go faster and see what he does.' The next time he bolted, I tried it and it worked. He only bolted because he knew he wasn't supposed to. If I called his bluff, he slowed down.

I'd had Jack for about eighteen months when we had all our tacks stolen from the stables. It was six months before I could afford another saddle, so I had to ride bareback until then. It was difficult to stay on, but it taught me to ride better. Without a saddle, you can feel the horse and feel what it's thinking. It's the same with Ted now: when he's leaning against me, I know what he's going to do next from the way his body feels. In hindsight, riding bareback wasn't the best idea, but riding was the only thing that made me happy.

Jack was a little horror – and I loved him to bits. It was his spirit I loved. He was stubborn and he liked to do things in his own way – like me, I suppose. And underneath it all, he was very loyal. They were the same qualities, much later in life, that I would love about Ted.

chapter 3

A Mistake that Nearly Cost My Life

It was May 1970 and I had just turned twenty-one. I was happy. I was working for the Ministry of Transport now, at the motorway planning centre. Rose and I were still great friends – we went everywhere together. She'd come out with me when I went riding and ride her bike alongside Jack. We went to dances together and we joined the church choir where she lived.

I was slowly becoming more confident: I'd got a boyfriend and he'd persuaded me to stop wearing gloves on my hands every time I went out. Eventually, we broke up when he got offered a job in New Zealand. Before he left, he turned up on my doorstep and asked me to emigrate with him. All I could think was that Jack wouldn't cope without me. Eventually, he said, 'You care more about your horse than you do about me!' I didn't know what to say – I couldn't tell him he was wrong, so he stormed off and that was the end of that. But the confidence he'd given me stayed with me and I was finally able to go out in public with my hands showing.

Rose had got married and was living in Shropshire, where her husband, Malcolm, was studying at an agricultural college. I had gone to visit them with a new boyfriend and one day, when the men had gone out together, Rose and I made dinner for us all. We decided to make a curry. I was in charge of putting the curry powder in but I misread the recipe: I tipped a tablespoon into the pan, when it should only have been a teaspoon. It was a mistake that would nearly cost me my life.

We sat down to eat. It was the first time Rose and I had cooked together and everyone was joking that it was going to poison us. 'OK, well, I'll try it first then,' I said and I took a mouthful. Instantly, the burning curry took the skin off the interior of my mouth. Malcolm had taken a tiny mouthful at the same time and he immediately grabbed his water glass – I could see him guzzling it, but it was too late. I was too embarrassed to spit it out so I swallowed it. A huge black blister filled my throat and mouth, I couldn't swallow and it became hard to breathe. Rose called 999.

For most people, calling 999 is straightforward: you know you'll get help. For people with EB, calling 999 is where our problems begin. So few nurses or doctors have heard of it and they can end up doing more harm than good. Ordinary procedures can cause huge amounts of damage – handling us or removing our clothes can cause blisters, and plasters can take the skin off. I know much more about my condition than they do, but they often don't listen when I tell them that they can't do something.

When I went to A & E in 1970, they decided to perform a tracheotomy. I was terrified: I was away from home and my parents had no idea I was in hospital or the kind of danger I was in. I had the pre-med but just as I was being wheeled into the operating theatre, the huge blister in my throat and mouth burst. The pain was awful and they called off the operation. I was lucky: later, I was told by a specialist that a tracheotomy would have been extremely risky for someone with my skin condition and I could easily have died.

The burst blister left folds of skin in my throat that would be the cause of problems for many years to come. I found it almost impossible to swallow. Even liquid hurt to drink. I could hardly eat anything at all as my throat had become partly blocked, so I lost a huge amount of weight and was admitted to hospital for months.

I was diagnosed as anorexic: they thought that I didn't want to eat, not that I couldn't. I can still remember one doctor slamming a plate of fish and chips down on the tray at the end of my bed. 'I will never give into you,' he said.

One night, my mother came to visit me in hospital. I was talking to her about my childhood and I could see her getting steadily more anxious. Then suddenly, she got up and went out of the room. I didn't understand why she was leaving me. The next morning I was taken by ambulance to Guy's Hospital in London.

It turned out she'd thought I was about to die – when I'd started talking about my childhood she'd thought it was my life flashing before my eyes, so she'd gone to track down the first doctor I'd seen in London, the doctor who'd said it was OK to let me ride, because he at least understood what was wrong with me. She said to him, 'She didn't stop! You told me she'd stop riding if she got hurt, but she didn't! She didn't stop!'

At Guy's, they put me on intravenous fluids and gave me a barium swallow, a test where you swallow a liquid that shows any problems with the oesophagus under X-ray. I could hardly manage to get it down, but when I did, the doctors could see that two webs of skin from the blister had grown across my throat. I remember the doctor bringing a group of students to see me on the ward and banging the tray at the end of my bed. 'Always remember,' he said, 'when someone with EB says there is something in their throat, that means there *is* something in their throat.'

The next day they operated to dilate my oesophagus. It was one of the worst things I've ever gone through. I knew it had to be done: I was twenty-one, and five-and-a-half stone. I was clearly dying. But it was a horrible experience.

I was told I would be operated on by a surgeon who had performed the operation before, but at the last minute, he was called away. They asked another doctor but he refused to do it. He came to see me and said, 'I've been asked to do your operation, but only someone with a gun to their head or completely drunk would attempt it. I'm sorry – I just can't risk your life.'

In the end, they found a surgeon to do it and I remember singing as I was wheeled off to be operated on – I'd made friends with the girls on the ward and I knew they were worried about me. I was trying to cheer them up. When I came round, there was blood everywhere. They'd forced a tube down my throat to open it and removed all the skin – the pain was horrendous.

I had the operation on 10 December and I was finally out of hospital a few days before Christmas. It saved my life, but it was six months before I could swallow without pain. My throat never recovered properly. To this day, I can't be in a room with curry or garlic without my throat swelling.

The doctor I saw after the operation told me that there were two things I'd never do: 'You won't be able to sing or cry.' Although the operation had dilated my throat it would never be a normal size, and if I did either of those things, my throat would contract and damage the skin. I had to stop going to choir and I still can't show any emotion: good or bad. If I want to cry, I have to distract myself or my throat will contract and cause terrible problems. They said they might even have to operate again, but I swore I would never put myself through it a second time.

I was also told I might live for only two more years. Another deadline. I think it made me stronger. I became more determined than ever to make each day count.

chapter 4

Second Time Lucky

By January 1971 I was back at work. It was just a month after my operation and I was still very thin and poorly, but I was determined to get back to leading a normal life. The doctor wouldn't sign me back to work – he said I wasn't well enough. Work said they couldn't pay me since I wasn't supposed to be there, but they let me go in anyway. I'd broken up with my boyfriend, but I was still firm friends with Rose. In February we went together to a Valentine's Day dance at work. It was there that I met my first husband. We were married just five months later, and five years later I gave birth to my first child.

I had always been told that I couldn't have children. Not because I might pass on my condition – by this time I understood the genetic factors and I knew that the chances of passing it on were very, very small. EB is rare and the kind that I have – the recessive kind – is even rarer: both parents have to have the defective gene to pass it on. But the doctors weren't sure how my body would cope with pregnancy and birth, and advised me not to try for a baby.

By then, I knew that I didn't have to listen if someone told me I shouldn't do something. I wanted a child. Rose was pregnant and in those days having children was something that was expected of you. It was part of having a normal life and I wanted that for myself.

My first pregnancy passed without too many complications. I started to bleed at eleven weeks and thought I was losing the baby, but I was told he hadn't adhered to the side of the womb properly. I had to lie down for three weeks and the rest of the pregnancy was fine. I got through labour, too, without complications. I was supposed to have the baby in London, where I could be monitored by specialists, but I ended up having him in Wales where we were living at the time. They could give me nothing for the pain as they didn't know how my body would react, so I only had breathing exercises. I had a French midwife, and she told me to look out of the window and blow on the bluebells as if they were candles I was trying to blow out. I became very controlled, very focused, and I managed the pain. It was a long labour, but after fifteen hours, my healthy baby boy, Robert, was born. I was so thrilled I thought I would burst. He was so beautiful.

When he was three, it seemed the right time to try for another baby. Because it had been OK with Robert, I was confident that my body could cope with another pregnancy and labour. This time it was more difficult. I was four and a half months pregnant when, as I was getting Robert ready for playschool, I had the most awful pains. I rang a friend and she called an ambulance. The ambulance took me to hospital and I was told I had gone into labour early. I would have to spend the next four and a half months lying in bed in hospital to avoid labour until the baby was ready to be born.

I couldn't stand the thought of being apart from Robert for so long, so I told the doctor I would have to go home. He assured me that Robert wouldn't remember: 'If you ask him, when he's older, how long you were away for, he'll say, "Just one day".' Sure enough, when we asked him later, that's what he said. But I missed him so much. The time dragged and mothers came and went over the long months. A lady said she was going to call her baby girl after me and hope her child was as patient as I was. I don't consider myself a patient person – I just had to try and save my baby.

People had said to me that complications in pregnancy were sometimes nature's way of getting rid of the baby if there was something wrong with it. I started having nightmares about the birth, dreaming that the baby would be born with blisters. When my daughter Rhiannon was born, the doctors picked her up straight away and took her away from me. I felt like I'd been shot. They turned away, took her to one end of the room and nobody spoke. I thought then that she had EB. I was totally devastated.

Luckily, Rhiannon was fine. She was adorable. Absolutely amazing. Two healthy babies. I was over the moon.

It was a challenge to do the things other mums took for granted. It was difficult to do up buttons or play rough games, and the children had to learn that they couldn't climb all over me: they couldn't climb on my knee or jump and bounce on me.

Once, when Robert was a baby, a woman snatched him away from me in the clinic, shouting, 'How could you? How could you?' I realised that my hands had been bleeding when I was doing up his Babygro and he was covered in blood – she thought I'd attacked him. It took ages to convince her it was my blood not his. She was very apologetic afterwards but it made me realise just how careful I had to be.

I was determined Robert and Rhiannon wouldn't miss out on anything because of me. I think they had a happy childhood. We had dogs and ponies. My aunty Gwen had given me a golden retriever, Topper, as a wedding present, and my husband and I rehomed rescue dogs. Both children rode horses and loved the outdoors. They were strong and able. They did all the things I longed to do and it made me smile to watch them. It was like watching myself with normal skin. I am immensely proud of them both.

My first husband and I divorced in 1990. After the divorce, things were difficult: I was on my own with two children of fourteen and ten, and I was very low.

It was a hard time and I think I only got through it with the help of good friends. I stopped riding my horse, Kestrel, and my friend Mavis looked after him while I got back on my feet – she was really kind. One day, she turned up at my gate on her horse, Brandy, leading Kestrel with his tack on. She rang the doorbell and I came out to see her standing by my gate with two horses. She said, 'Kestrel needs you to ride him. Come on, let's go out together.' And I did. She knew I had to ride to be happy. She helped me keep my sanity. I could only think clearly when I relaxed on my horse.

During this time, my EB nurse asked me to picture my dream future. I said I could see a little house with a dog on the veranda, where I lived with my children and bred dogs. I was still mad about dogs. I now had a beautiful golden retriever called Heidi. She was the gentlest dog you could meet and I adored her.

'Go for it,' my nurse said, when I told her. 'Have that goal in your mind and just do it.' I told her I had no intention of marrying again – all I wanted was my children, the house and the dogs. Luckily, life doesn't always go as planned. Sometimes, it has good things up its sleeve.

One day, I was on my own with the children and my friend Judy rang to see how I was. I said I could do with some adult company. I'd given up work when I got married and, although I'd always wanted to go back, at that point it was more than I could cope with. It was hard being at home all day. Judy told me she went to a singles group and suggested I go along with her.

'Oh no, you can forget that,' I said. 'I'm never getting married again.'

'It's not like that,' she said. 'It's social not romantic. It's a Christian singles group – a group of us get together and visit different churches and go to the theatre together, things like that. It's just for company.'

That sounded like something I could manage.

The next meeting was a Christmas dinner in a beautiful restaurant with a conservatory. It was snowing and there was an old-fashioned lamp-post outside. The snow drifted past the light, falling steadily, and I thought of Narnia. I found I enjoyed getting out of the house and meeting new people. It had been good for me. And there was a man called Peter who seemed particularly nice.

I started going out with the group regularly. Peter and I and another man called Stephen would take it in turns to drive each other to the events. We'd go to churches with dwindling congregations to try to swell the numbers and give them a bit of encouragement to keep going.

On one trip, to Lavenham in Suffolk, we were walking through the fields before the evening service at church. I can't walk very fast, so I was always at the back of the group. As we passed a pond I stopped to look at the ducklings on the water. I assumed everyone had gone on ahead and I'd catch them up at the church. 'Oh, aren't you sweet!' I said to the ducklings.

'They are pretty, aren't they?' said a voice behind me. I turned round and saw that Peter was there. He'd waited for me.

We arrived at the church for the evening service. It was freezing inside – I've never been so cold. I sat in the pew looking up at its beautiful stained glass window, which showed a white horse rearing up.

'I'd love that,' I said.

'I'll get it for you, soon as the church shuts,' Peter said and I smiled. Then, when he saw how cold I was, he put his jacket round my shoulders. Something clicked. It felt so nice. But I was afraid of how nice it felt. I didn't want to get hurt again.

The next time, Peter asked me to go for a walk with him on his own and I agreed. I enjoyed his company – he was so nice and so sweet. We became friends. I invited him to Robert's birthday party to meet the children. When I answered Peter's ring at the doorbell, we heard a huge crash from inside the house, and rushed through to find glass all over the floor. The boys had kicked a football through the window. Robert had gone white.

'Right, where's your dustpan and brush?' Peter said. 'Don't worry, Robert – I expect your mum's insured.' Robert couldn't believe it. Peter was so kind and calm, exactly as he's been throughout our marriage.

He was good with Rhiannon too. When her hamster was ill, Peter rushed over to our house to be with her. Sadly, it died and he helped her bury it in the garden. We sang a hymn and prayed for it. Losing an animal is so hard at any age and Rhiannon was devastated. I realised then how kind Peter was and how well he got on with the children. Later on, Rhiannon asked Peter if he would be her part-time dad.

One day he suggested we go back to Lavenham together. I went out riding with Mavis the day before and told her what we were doing.

'He's going to ask you to marry him, you know.'

'Oh, don't be so stupid!'

'Well, why's he taking you all the way to Lavenham then?'

'Because he wants to go to Lavenham!' I said.

I didn't believe a word of Mavis's prediction. But when we got there, we walked the same way we had the first time we went there with the group, Peter stopped at the pond where the ducklings had been and, sure enough, asked me to marry him. I burst out laughing. I just couldn't believe that Mavis had been right.

'What's so funny?' he said.

I turned serious. 'I'm sorry,' I said. 'I'd love to marry you, but I have decided to never, ever get married again.'

'I know,' Peter said. 'But I also know that we could be happy together.'

I looked at him and I thought, *You are the nicest man I have ever met*. I knew I loved him.

I said yes. Peter told me later that he knew I was the woman he was going to marry the very first time he saw me at the restaurant.

We decided to wait a few days before telling the children – we wanted to find the right moment. But the next time Peter came round to visit, we were saying prayers with Rhiannon at bedtime and she opened her eyes and asked, 'Will you be my full-time dad?' Peter and I just looked at each other and smiled.

The next day, there was a lot of giggling and I was told to keep out of the kitchen and the dining room. Peter had secretly told them that we were going to be a family. When Peter arrived that night they showed us they had made an engagement cake to surprise us.

The children were delighted, but the real judge was Heidi, my dog. Peter had never had dogs, and before he first visited the house I was worried he might not like her and vice versa. In fact, Heidi fell in love with him instantly and he took over from me as her best friend. She idolised him and loved him coming to see us. 'But Heidi, you're *my* dog!' I'd say. *Sorry, I've got Peter now*, she'd say as she trotted towards him. 'You little traitor!' I'd reply.

We married later that year, in 1991, and we're still as happy now as the day we met. Peter is kind and gentle and great fun to be with, and he's seen me through some very difficult times. He has given me security in an uncertain world. He works tirelessly to make our lives a better place. He really is the wind beneath my wings.

He is always strong for me and helps but never hinders. He knows me well enough not to say I cannot do things I set my heart on.

Over time, my condition got slowly worse. After the operation in 1970, I had to be very careful what I ate and eat only soft food. I didn't learn, though; I still tried to eat things they said I shouldn't. In 1993, I choked on a piece of cheese. It did a huge amount of damage to my throat, and after that the doctor said I shouldn't be left alone when I was eating – I could choke at any time or, worse still, I could get pneumonia. Peter had to give up work to care for me.

It was around this time that I learnt I was allergic to oilseed rape – even just the smell can cause blisters in my mouth and throat. We had to move several times to avoid it. As soon as we settled anywhere, someone would start growing it near us and we would have to move again. I tried wearing a mask but it didn't help. The repeated blistering of my throat was causing webbing and shrinking it. I ended up on very soft food.

The doctors advised us to move right away from the oilseed rape and try to live on the coast, so we moved to Aldeburgh in Suffolk in 1998. We took Heidi, but I left Max, my horse, behind with my daughter. Rhiannon was grown-up now and had been riding him as much as I had, but she had just got a new job and didn't have time to see him every day. We decided to put him out on loan until one of us could take him back. Max had arthritis in his back leg and couldn't go up any slopes – we explained to his new carers that he had to be on level ground at all time.

Not long after we moved, I had a phone call from the people that were looking after him telling me that Max had been put down. I was horrified. He'd been left in a field surrounded by a ditch – he'd climbed into it and hadn't been able to get out. When the fire brigade got him out, he was in shock and couldn't stand. The vet had to shoot him.

I was heartbroken. Two weeks later, Heidi died of cancer. We were devastated. The next six months were extremely difficult. I'd hit a low. I didn't go out and I certainly didn't speak to anyone. I was becoming more and more introverted and I'd completely lost confidence in myself. My nerves were bad; I was a nervous wreck. I realised then what a big part animals had played in my happiness.

Then I got the phone call that would change my life.

'Can you rehome two four-year-old golden retrievers?'

chapter 5

Monty and Penny

'I've found two rescue dogs, golden retrievers, that need a home. But they need it right now.'

The call came from a friend of ours who lived nearby – he knew how devastated we'd been to lose Heidi and how much I loved golden retrievers. After Heidi, we couldn't envisage life with another dog, so we'd decided not to get one, but we were starting to realise what a mistake that was. Having Heidi had meant walks and visits. Now we were in Aldeburgh and we didn't know anyone – I didn't know how to interact with people without a dog. We'd just been starting to think that we ought to get another dog – our friend had rung at exactly the right time.

'I can take one, but not two,' I said. 'We can't manage two dogs, not at the moment.'

'You don't understand, Wendy,' he said. 'They have to stay together. You can't separate them. You'll understand when you see them.'

'Well, OK, we'll go and have a look at them,' I said. 'But I can't promise we'll be able to take them.' I put the phone down and wondered what on earth Peter would think of us having two dogs together. My friend had also told me that they had not had much, if any, training.

'Let's go and see them,' Peter said. 'You never know, they might be quieter than you think!'

One look at them was all it took. We were taken to a car park behind a restaurant and shown a tiny pen with two dogs inside: a smaller greyish brown bitch and a darker male. Their coats were dreadfully matted and the male had a wound on his leg that was bleeding. There was dog poo on the floor of the kennel and flies were gathering round. They were both dreadfully over-weight, like puddings on legs.

'Well, they're not golden retrievers, for a start,' I said. I thought of aunty Gwen's beautiful animals with their soft gleaming coats. These dogs were nothing like them.

'What are they, then?' Peter asked.

'I don't know,' I said. 'Their fur's so matted I can't tell.'

We took them out for a walk, to see how we got on with them. They were so eager to go with us, they greeted us like long lost friends. As soon as we'd got them out of the pen, they dragged us down the road. It was clear then that they had had no training whatso-ever – nothing we said had any influence on their behaviour. There was a dried up old leather lead in the kennel, but they obviously had no idea what it was for. They were so wilful that Peter struggled to hold on to them both.

When we took them back to the kennel they stubbornly refused to go back in. I knew then that it was too late – it would have been cruel to leave them. I turned to Peter and said, 'We're having them both. We've got to.'

'I know,' he said.

The owners didn't want them any more – they were quite happy for us to take them there and then. They didn't even ask where were taking them. We got the dogs to the car, and as soon as we opened the door they jumped straight in. Just as we were about to drive off, I remembered that I'd brought a photo album with pictures of our house, so the owners could see the dogs' new home. I tried to get the dogs out again, so we could go back and show their owners the album, but now they were in the car they refused to get out.

'This isn't a very good sign, is it?' I said to Peter, as we drove off. The dogs didn't once look back at their owners.

On the drive back from the kennel we took them to the vet. He told us that they were two-and-a-half stone overweight. He said the male dog was so fat his heart could give up at any moment. They would have to go on a diet for months. Their teeth were worn down from chewing on the bars of the kennel, trying to get out. The female had a huge black scar on her neck – we found out later that she had been tied up when she was in season to stop her running away. The wire had taken all the fur off. The vet said it would never grow back.

We asked him to microchip them and he laughed. 'I don't think anyone's going to want to steal these two!'

Our emotions on the way home were mixed – we already cared deeply for these two dogs, but I was anxious. Here we were with two untrained dogs, overweight and wilful, and I had delicate skin. They weren't even golden retrievers. But they were already looking up at us so lovingly – it was impossible to resist. I was already head over heels in love.

We got back home and took them into the kitchen. We took off their leads and they just stood there. To this day, I will never forget the look that passed between them. They looked round the room, then at each other, and then slowly wagged their tails. I could see them saying to each other: *We've made it – we're home!* I wanted to cry.

Already, on our first walk together, they'd chosen their owners: Penny would go with Peter and Monty would go with me.

We took them round to see our neighbour, an elderly lady who loved dogs. 'Oh my goodness!' she said, when she saw what a state they were in. But she was particularly taken with Penny, who she called 'the little brown dog'.

'What on earth are you going to do with them?' she asked.

'Well, they're going to the dog groomers, for a start,' I said.

There was no way we could sort their matted coats out on our own. We dropped the dogs off at the groomers in town at 8.30 a.m. the next day. I was a nervous wreck all day. I couldn't help worrying about how they were coping – I just wanted them at home. I drove Peter mad, constantly asking him what the time was. Finally, at 3.30 p.m., seven hours after we'd left them, the phone rang. They were ready to be picked up.

We arrived at the groomers and there was no sign of Monty and Penny. I felt disloyal, but I couldn't help noticing two resplendent golden retrievers tied up at the front of the shop, one almost white and one pale gold. They looked beautiful, just how golden retrievers should look. I felt a pang – I'd seen my heart's desire, but I couldn't have it. I couldn't stop staring at them.

The dog groomer was out the back, so I called out to her. 'It's us! We've come for Monty and Penny!'

She called back, 'The dogs are there – won't be a minute!'

'No, I don't think so,' I said. 'There's just two goldens out front, and whoever owns them will not appreciate me taking them, I can tell you!'

The lady appeared from the back. 'They're your dogs!' she said, laughing.

'I wish they were!'

'Well, they're the ones you brought in at 8.30 a.m. this morning,' she said. 'And if they hadn't been so good-natured we would have had to shave all their fur off, it was so matted. It's taken five baths, but we managed to wash and brush them. And here they are!'

I was astounded. They were absolutely unrecognisable. It was like a magic trick. We had dropped off two dogs, one brown and one grey, both of unknown breed, and in front of us stood the prettiest, sweetest golden retrievers you could ever meet. The dogs could tell how astonished we are – I knew they were laughing at us.

On the way home, we saw our neighbour. 'Oh, what a shame!' she said. 'What happened to your little brown dog?'

'This is her!' I said, pointing at Penny, who was now pure white.

'That's not the dog you brought in last night. Where's your little brown dog? The one you rescued?'

She refused to believe they were the same animals. From that day on, every time she saw us, she'd ask us what happened to our little brown dog.

chapter 6

The Perfect Puppies

The next day, the fun began. We put Monty and Penny on leads and planned to take them to Peter's mother's house, which was only round the corner, but it soon became clear that we wouldn't even get that far. They were stubborn dogs and they had no intention of walking with us. They were so overweight they couldn't run, but Penny could trot and Monty could walk fast. As soon as we got out of the door, they set off as fast as they could in different directions, pulling me and Peter along behind them. They pulled on the leads so hard that even Peter had to let go. There was no question of 'stay' or 'heel': they did exactly what they wanted.

'OK,' I said. 'They're going to need lessons.'

We took them to a local dog trainer, who ran classes in the village hall. We arrived at their first class and they rushed into the hall like they were on a supermarket trolley dash. All the other dog owners had to get out of their way as they zoomed around the room, knocking things over, bumping into people and refusing to do anything they were told.

Penny was definitely the ringleader. She always wanted to do hundreds of things at once: *Come on, Monty, let's say hello to that dog! And what's that over here? Come on, let's go and have a look at that dog over there!* We could see already that Monty was a quieter dog. He was following, but you could almost hear him pleading with her: *Penny, are you sure? Shouldn't we just do as we're told?*

The trainer was an ex-army man and believed in the old-fashioned training methods, where you pushed and pulled the dogs around to get them to behave. 'Tell her to sit!' he said to me, trying to push Penny's backside down with his hand. Penny wasn't having any of it. After a very fraught half hour we were asked to leave as our dogs were disrupting the class. I tried to explain that we'd rehomed them and we'd had them only a few days.

'Take them back,' the trainer said. 'You'll never train one, let alone two together. Don't try and keep them.'

We finally managed to get the dogs under control and out of the hall. We bundled them back into the car and sat in silence for a moment. 'So what happens now?' Peter asked.

I looked at Monty and Penny and my heart turned somersaults.

'They're not going back,' I said. 'I can't do it to them. We just need a new way of doing things. From now on, we're going to treat them like they're puppies. We need to pretend they're eight weeks old, not four and a half years. We'll call them our puppies and treat them just as we would an eight-week-old.'

Peter laughed. 'Why?'

'We need to start from scratch,' I said. 'Begin with simple things and build up. I don't know if it'll work but at least if we call them puppies, we won't expect too much.'

We decided we would start by training them for ten minutes a day. The trouble was, as soon as we let them off the leads, they disappeared. Off they went, not a care in the world. We kept calling them back, but they kept going. I started to panic. What if they never came back?

Slowly, it dawned on me: it wasn't that they wanted to leave us, but they didn't see the point in coming back. They knew we were there, so they went off and did their own thing, safe in the knowledge we wouldn't leave them. So I decided to try something different.

'Next time we call them, we're going to hide behind the sand dunes,' I told Peter. 'We'll call them and then they'll turn round to look for us.'

'But they won't see us.'

'Exactly! Come on.'

I don't know where I got the idea from. Just instinct, I think. It was no good carrying on calling them: they weren't listening anyway, so what was the point? I wanted them to be a bit shocked when they turned round and discovered we weren't there.

'Monty! Penny! Come on, time to go home!' we called out. Then we hid. At first it was funny, the two of us crouched behind the sand dunes together. Then I began to worry. What if they never found us? What if they just ran out onto the road and hurt themselves? We were about give up and look for them when we heard the jangle of the tags on their collars. Then we were showered with sand – they could smell us, but they didn't know where we were and were scrabbling around the dune trying to find us.

All of a sudden, we were ambushed. It was like being caught in a sandstorm. Slobbery kisses covered our hands and faces. You could see how relieved they were to find us. And then they sat on us! We couldn't stop laughing. Two overweight dogs, pleased to see us again, were lying on top of us and we couldn't get up.

But the plan had worked: they never ran off again. When we called them, they would turn round to check we were there. I learned a new trick too: if I wanted them to come back, I would call them and then turn round and go the other way. Penny and Monty would look round, thinking, *Oh that's OK, they're still there*, but then when they saw me walking away from them, they'd race after me. And, from there, they learnt they had to come back when they were called.

Before the dogs had come into our lives, we'd enrolled in a course at the Suffolk Wildlife Trust. We didn't want to miss it, so we decided they'd be OK on their own for just a few hours. We shut them in the kitchen, so they couldn't get up to too much mischief, and set off.

We loved the class: it was taught on a beautiful nature reserve, the tutor was brilliant, and the volunteers and classmates were lovely. But when we arrived home in good spirits, we found two very stressed dogs and no kitchen carpet. They'd dug up the carpet and chewed it to pieces.

'What do we do now?' said Peter. 'Do they get smacked?'

'No, they never get smacked,' I said. I'd never trained an animal by punishment – I'd never even carried a whip on a horse. My dad said to me once, 'If you always carry a whip, the day you drop the whip, the horse is going to play you up because you haven't got the thing that's kept it under control. Always remember, if you're ever not nice to something, it will find a way to pay you back.' But, besides that, it isn't needed. I don't believe anyone or anything learns by punishment.

But we needed some way to show them it wasn't a good idea. We decided to show our disapproval by ignoring them. Whatever they did, we would not acknowledge them.

They were beside themselves. After an hour or two, we couldn't do it any more: we decided it was only a carpet and fed them their tea. But it worked. Thankfully, they never did anything like that again.

Clearly, leaving them on their own was not an option. I rang the Wildlife Trust and explained we had two new 'puppies' that couldn't be left, so we couldn't go to any more classes.

'No problem,' the tutor said. 'Bring them along. They can stay out on the veranda while you're in the class. Bring water and beds and see how they are. It would be lovely to have two puppies here.'

Now we had a deadline! They were going to need a lot more training before they could sit quietly outside a classroom for an hour. We needed to teach them 'stay', so they could be apart from us and not worry we were abandoning them.

Next day, off we went to train them. The most popu-lar method of training at that time was very physical, the way the trainer at the dog school had behaved: pull on the lead to get them to stop, push their backside down to get them to sit, pull on their paws to get them to lie down. That had never been an option for me – it seemed cruel and would have been too hard on my skin. We did it by rewarding them with treats when they did as we asked, and ignoring them if they didn't obey us.

Training dogs by reward alone works, but you have to be very patient. We let go of their leads, got their attention and asked for the stay. But when we walked forward, so did they. OK, so now what? One small step at a time. Ask them to stay, take a small step forward and go back and reward them if they 'stayed'. It seemed to take a lifetime. Penny was the first to 'stay'. We'd managed to get her to sit, and then Peter said to her, 'You sit there and wait, I'm just going over here.' She stayed sitting but you could see the concern on her face: *You're not going far?* 'I'm not going far,' Peter reassured her. *You're not going to leave me forever?* 'I'm not going to leave you forever.' He stood back. Penny stayed where she was and looked up at him. *Like this?* 'That's it, good girl!'

We were over the moon. We rewarded her with treats and made a huge fuss of her. You could see it dawning on her: *Oh, I see: you mean sit here while you go there! Well, why didn't you say?* Monty copied her straight away – he was never one to miss an opportunity for food! Bit by bit, we built it up so they would stay for longer and longer. Finally, we had two 'staying puppies'.

'Where are the puppies?' the tutor asked, when we arrived at college the next week with two relatively well-behaved four-year-old dogs. We explained why we called them puppies and he laughed. In all our time attending classes, they were no bother at all. They never made a sound. They loved being fussed over at tea break and Monty even let a three-year-old boy walk him on a lead. Penny was still too erratic – she was always a dizzy blonde!

All break times were spent with our classmates sitting on the veranda with coffees and talking to the dogs. Afterwards we would take them for a good walk by the river. They were getting happier and healthier by the minute.

We tried really hard with their diets and they eventually reached their perfect weight. I can still remember the first time they ran. We were visiting friends who also had two golden retrievers – the dogs were best friends with Monty and Penny and they spent their birthdays together. We took the dogs into the paddock at the back of our friends' house and I called for them. Monty came to find me, running like a two-year-old. It was so moving. The fur had grown back on Penny's neck, where the wire had hurt her. And they were so good-natured – typical golden retrievers. It became clear we had two very special dogs. We were about to find out just how special.

chapter 7

Rags to Riches

Monty and Penny went from strength to strength and we loved them more and more each day. They had very different personalities. Penny was always a bit aloof, however much training she'd had: if you told her to do something, she wouldn't do it straight away. *I'll do it in a minute, if I've got time, if it's convenient.* She certainly wasn't going to do it if you tried to make her! She was independent, really – headstrong. She'd start digging up the garden and we'd call out to her: 'Penny, don't do that!' And she'd run round in a circle, then go and dig somewhere else. *Well, you just said I couldn't do it over there! I can do it over here.* 'No, Penny, you can't do it *anywhere*!'

Monty was the opposite. He needed so much re-assurance. He always wanted to hug and cuddle. He was gentle and loyal to a fault. If he'd been human, he would have been a man with a suit, a bowler hat and an umbrella, and he'd have tipped his hat to you and said,

'Good morning, madam, lovely day.' He was a pure gentleman. Penny was more of a rogue!

We took the dogs everywhere with us – they even came on holiday with us. On one holiday, to Scotland, we took them on the train. They were big dogs and they didn't fit under the seat. The ticket lady came past and we said apologetically that there was no room for them. 'Well,' she said. 'We're just going to have to move you to first class.'

First class was wonderfully luxurious. The staff were so taken with the dogs and gave them five-star treatment. The ticket lady asked if she could take them for a walk along the train – she'd only got to the end of the carriage when Penny spotted her first picnic basket and started sniffing for food. Then they worried that the dogs were getting too hot, so they turned down the heating on the entire train! As we sat at the table with little lamps on it, being brought food and drink, I laughed as I remembered the miserable little kennel Monty and Penny had come from. They really had gone from rags to riches.

Peter and I love cycling, so Peter built Monty and Penny a cage on wheels to go behind his bicycle. At first they were both too scared to get in it, so I threw cheese biscuits into the cage and they leapt in. Food always overturned their fears!

We took it on holiday to Padstow with us. Peter is shy by nature, so I couldn't believe it when he rode his bike around a car park with Monty and Penny in the cage on wheels behind him. It brought the car park to a standstill. People laughed and clapped, and Monty and Penny seemed to laugh as well.

We started to volunteer at a horticultural therapy garden near Aldeburgh. Horticultural therapy gardens are for people who are disabled, isolated or vulnerable – it's a place where they can meet people and learn practical skills and experience the joy of growing their own plants. Peter built garden furniture for a living before he gave up work to care for me, so he built benches and taught classes and I grew plants. We sold them at shows to raise funds to keep the garden going.

We'd take the dogs with us. They loved it and everyone loved seeing them. One day I couldn't find Penny anywhere, so I went off to look for her. I searched and searched. They had been so good about not running off, I was surprised she'd gone. I decided to go to the office building to see if she was there. As I passed the office I could see her looking out of the window. When I opened the door, I saw she was sitting on the boss's swivel chair. I don't know what she thought she was doing. She just wagged her tail and looked angelic.

The training went so well that we decided to register Monty and Penny as Pets As Therapy (PAT) dogs. Pets As Therapy is a charity that arranges for people to bring their pets to visit hospitals, hospices and care homes, to spread some of the companionship, joy and unconditional love that only an animal can bring.

To be registered the animals have to pass various assessments. They have to have the right kind of personality – they have to be calm and well trained, and happy to meet lots of different people. We filled in all the forms and were so excited when a letter arrived to arrange a date for their test, but I was a little bit nervous. We still remembered the wild and wilful dogs we'd brought home from the kennel!

But on the day of the test, Monty and Penny behaved beautifully. Handling them was fine. Walking nicely went well. Then they had to check they were not startled by sudden noises. Monty went first and I set off along the path with him. BANG! They dropped a metal tray behind me. I jumped out of my skin. Monty remained calm. The same thing happened with Penny. When the final report came back, it said: 'Dogs passed marvellously – owner failed!'

We began to visit elderly folks' homes and hospitals. Monty and Penny would work the room between them: one would go round the room one way and one the other way. Everyone loved them and it was a pleasure to see how much joy they brought.

At one home, I was warned that there was a lady who couldn't hear or speak. I approached her cautiously with Monty, ready to leave if she gave any indication of not wanting to see him. Instead, she touched his ear and said, 'So soft.' I told her Monty's name and again she said, 'So soft.'

On the way out I told the staff – they couldn't believe it. One of the nurses took a book to the lady and asked her if she could read it. She read aloud in a beautiful voice. The nurse asked her why she had never spoken, and she said, 'I don't want to be here.' I wanted to cry. It reminded me of myself at boarding school.

Next time I visited she was chattering away and I was told they had moved her room and she was much happier. Without Monty's visit, I wonder how long it would have been before she'd spoken.

Another time, we visited a hospital and asked if there were any rooms we shouldn't enter. They said to avoid one room with a family and a very ill, elderly lady. Later, as we were leaving, the door opened and a woman came out. She told me her mother was dying and seemed unresponsive. They had no idea if her mother could hear them or knew they were there, and she asked if I would take Monty to her bedside to see if she knew he was there. She said that her mother loved dogs and she was sure she would respond to him if she could. I took Monty in and got him to put his paw in the elderly lady's hand. As I closed her hand around his paw, she broke into a beautiful smile. It was incredibly moving. The family thanked Monty and me, and we left the room. We heard later that she had died shortly after; I was so happy that Monty had brought some joy to her to her final moments.

As a PAT dog, Monty was once asked to help a little boy at primary school who was so frightened of dogs that he would run out into the road rather than pass one. I had received a phone call from the little boy's headmaster to ask if I could take Monty to meet him and hopefully help him with his fears. I explained that I would start by walking past the playground every day before attempting to approach the child. It was so important not to let it look staged.

Monty was brilliant. We started by walking past the playground fence at playtime. After a few days, the children began to expect me and Monty, and after a few weeks, I stopped to say hello to them through the fence. The teachers were aware of my mission so they watched us from a distance.

One day, I made a point of asking Monty to say hello through the railings. He sat nicely and offered a paw to the children. I could see the child we had come to help. He was keeping well away from us.

We decided it was time for me and Monty to go into the playground, though we made sure to stay near the gate. The children were thrilled. I never looked at the frightened little boy. I wanted him to come to us. Each day we called in and Monty shook hands with some of the children. The group began to grow. They loved Monty and Monty loved meeting them. He learnt the time we visited and started to bring me his lead about ten minutes before we left. I was so pleased to see how much he enjoyed the children's company.

One playtime, a large group of children had gathered round and were patting Monty's fur. Then, in the midst of the group, I saw a hand reach out very slowly and cautiously towards Monty. The frightened little boy touched Monty's shoulder, quickly pulled back and disappeared. I didn't look up. Each day he got braver. Our patience paid off. Before long the child was sitting beside Monty, smiling at us and asking lots of questions about dogs. I couldn't have been more thrilled.

Later that day I had a phone call from the headmaster thanking us, and the next day, the little boy handed us a beautiful card. His parents had written to thank Monty for being such a wonderful dog. It had been our pleasure. We carried on walking by the playground to say hello to the children. The difference now was that *all* the children rushed to the railings to meet us.

We began to see that Monty had an effect on people that not all dogs had. One holiday in Padstow, he suddenly tried to pull away from me and cross the road. It made no sense – I couldn't see what he wanted on the other side. We were in the town centre and it was packed. Traffic everywhere. Monty was determined to cross the road and he kept pulling at his lead. He was a strong dog, I knew I wasn't going to be able to contain him much longer.

'You'll just have to follow him,' Peter said.

We crossed the road and Monty went straight towards a woman in a wheelchair and put his head on her knee. I tried to pull him away from her, but he insisted on staying there.

'I'm so sorry about this,' I said.

'Please don't stop him,' she said. 'I was willing him to come and see me. Our dog was put down two weeks ago and I really needed to cuddle your dog.'

To this day, I have no idea how he knew she needed him.

By this point, we'd moved to Devon – they were always growing new crops of oilseed rape, and my allergy kept us on the move. At our new house we had a lovely neighbour, an elderly lady, and I would always go round to see her and ask if she wanted any shopping done or help with anything. I would take the dogs in to say hello to her, and have a chat. Monty and Penny were very careful around her – I was so proud of them.

One Sunday, we were on our way to church when Monty started to pull towards her gate. I knew she visited her son on Sundays, so I tried to coax him away, but he wouldn't come. 'Monty, she's not there, she's gone out for the day!' I said. He still wouldn't move: he was leaning on the gate and trying to climb up it. 'For goodness sake, Monty!' I said. 'We're going to be late.' Peter had to lift him up and put him into the car.

I saw her the next day and told her about it. I thought she'd find it funny; instead, her face fell. 'Oh, I wish you'd rung the bell!' she said. 'I was too ill go out. I was here all on my own. I would have loved to have seen Monty.' I felt awful. I realised then that sometimes dogs know more than we do. I resolved that from that point on, the next time Monty told me something, I was going to listen.

chapter 8

Penny

Monty and Penny celebrated their ninth birthdays. We thought about how far they'd come from the scared, overweight dogs we'd seen in the kennel. They had given us so much love and brought so much happiness to the people around us.

Not long after their birthdays, we noticed that Penny was drinking lots of water. Too much. She wanted bowl after bowl. We made an appointment with the vet, thinking she'd picked up a virus or infection. Instead, we were told that it could be her kidneys. They ran tests and told us we'd have to wait for the results. It wasn't looking good.

After what seemed like weeks, the results came back, confirming she had kidney failure. They couldn't say how it had happened – they said she could have picked up some poison, maybe antifreeze. I couldn't understand how that would be possible. We'd always watched them closely.

Penny went to the vet to be put on a drip. Monty hated leaving her, just for a few hours. He paced the floor whining, while we cuddled him. Eventually we took him for a long walk to keep him busy. When she came home, he was beside himself with joy. He didn't understand that we might not have her back for long. Losing Penny was unbearable to think about. We put a duvet on the floor and all slept next to her. We lay on either side of her with our hands on her side, so we would wake up if she stirred.

I remember trying to stay awake for as long as I could because every moment with her was so precious. I didn't want to sleep through any of the time she had left. Monty was restless all the time. I looked forward to the nights, as it was the only time he lay still. By now, I think he knew that his beautiful sister was dying.

Slowly he refused food or to leave the house to go for anything but the toilet. Over the next few weeks, Penny spent more time in the vets than at home. She grew weaker every day. One morning she could barely stand.

Peter had a child's pushchair converted so she could still come on walks with us – he would push her along while she lay in it. She was so good, trying so hard to live for her dear Monty and us. We took her black-berrying along a canal path. Monty tried to stay as close to her as possible, walking with his head in the pushchair on Penny's side. He crooned to her.

Then one day she couldn't lift her head and I told Peter it was time. He couldn't bear it – he cried into her fur and begged her to keep going. I sent Peter to the shops for milk we didn't need and I called the vet. While we waited, I sang the 23rd Psalm to her with tears streaming down my face.

When the vet arrived, I took Monty over to a friend's. I couldn't bear for him to have to watch. He pulled at his lead when I tried to take him out – he didn't want to leave Penny's side. Finally I managed to get him to follow me.

Peter arrived home just as I did. 'Where are the puppies?' he asked. I took a deep breath and told him I had taken Monty to my friend's and that the vet was here, with Penny. He rushed in to see her and found the vet sitting on the floor with Penny's head on her lap. She was stroking her fur. She looked up at me and Peter.

'I think it's time to let Penny go,' she said.

We got out the puppies' photos albums and told the vet their story of rags to riches, from a filthy pen in a car park to hotels, holidays and a warm house with endless love.

In the end, we knew it had to happen. The vet inserted the needle to help Penny sleep and we all cried. The vet told us she'd gone almost immediately. She must have been ready to go.

It was a small comfort. We thanked her and she left us with Penny. Peter and I lay on the floor with her. Then, we covered her still body with a warm blanket and said tearful goodbyes. Peter started digging a hole for her in the garden. He was so distressed, he couldn't stop digging – it was deep enough for an elephant. We buried her with her collar and toys, her lead and a photo of Monty.

The house was too quiet. We both walked over to get Monty.

We had been so caught up in our own grief that we hadn't thought what it would do to Monty. He flew back to the house, bounded in the door and called out to Penny. His tail wagged furiously, as he searched every room. He asked to go in the garden and ran in circles whining. He stopped near the spot where Penny was buried. He sat by her grave and just hung his head.

After Penny had gone, Monty sank into a serious depression. We later learnt that we should have shown him Penny's body to help him come to terms with her death, but it was too late now. We were also devastated at losing Penny, so he would have absorbed our mourning as well. But he showed no signs of getting over it. Every day, he seemed to grieve more.

He started to give up on life. He didn't want to do anything. He wouldn't eat and didn't want to go for walks. He just kept looking for Penny. For weeks, when we came home from a walk, he would run into every single room. He was normally a quiet dog, but he barked loudly in each room. Then he'd come back to find us, sit down and stare at us, making a terrible, mournful sound. We knew that if he was human, he'd be sobbing.

Then he'd go and sit by her grave. I don't know what was going through his head – he must have known somehow that she was gone, because he knew where she was buried. But it was as if every time we came home, he had to search the house for her and go through the awful process of remembering her death.

He was so distraught that we never left him alone. We tried tempting him with all kinds of food, but it wasn't enough to keep him going. The vet started to get worried about him: he thought he might just waste away. After a while, we got worried too.

It was heartbreaking to watch. I thought that I was going to lose my precious Monty as well.

During this time, my throat had got progressively worse. My allergy to oilseed rape was causing prob-lems – even the slightest exposure to it caused more blisters on my throat and more scarring, making it diffi-cult to eat and speak. It seemed a good idea to learn British Sign Language (BSL), so that Peter and I could sign on days I could not speak. The only problem was that my hands were not very mobile – they had scarred badly and the skin had shrunk, and my fingers were closing in. I was offered an operation to straighten them, but it wasn't pleasant. A man who'd had it told me it had taken nine months before he could use his hands again after the operation.

I tried wearing splints to straighten them. I had to wear them for eight hours a day – one on one hand for four hours in the morning and one on the other hand for four hours in the afternoon. I couldn't wear them at night, in case I knocked the skin on my face with them. I hated having to do everything one-handed and I couldn't bear relying on Peter to do the things I couldn't.

One evening, it was time to take my splints off and Peter was outside – I couldn't take them off by myself and I couldn't open the door to go and get him. I've always been independent and I hate having to wait for someone to help me. If I can find a way to do something myself, then I will. I looked at Monty and I had an idea.

'Can you get that?' I said to Monty, showing him the Velcro fastener that held my splints in place. I tapped the Velcro fastener and asked him to tug it. He touched it with his nose. 'Tug, tug,' I said. He still didn't understand what I was asking him to do. I kept tapping it. In the end, he got hold of the Velcro in his mouth and I pulled my arm away so it came undone. Monty loved the noise the Velcro made. Once he knew that that was the result, he wanted to do it again.

Monty loved the new game – as soon as I put the splints on, he'd want to take them off again. I taught him to wait for the cue, and once he'd learnt it, I only had to say 'tug' and he'd undo them straight away. Then he wanted to take off everything with Velcro fasteners. My shoes also have Velcro fasteners; he learnt to undo them with his teeth and then pull off the shoe with his mouth.

It was helpful to have him do these little tasks for me, but the most rewarding thing was seeing the effect it had on him. It was the first time Monty had been excited by anything since Penny died. Slowly, his bounce started to return. The new game was to be the making of Monty – and me.

chapter 9

Monty Starts to Help

The more Monty helped, the happier he became. I started to teach him more and more, and he learnt ever so quickly. Soon, he was helping me take my jumpers off, and my trousers and my socks. He picked things up for me and even learnt to empty the washing machine. Peter would have to open the door for him – I never imagined that a dog could do that – but he'd pull the washing out with his mouth and drag it into the basket. He would pick up and carry his lead, take off my jacket, carry the shopping and help carry things around the house. He took notes to Peter and collected the post. We had great fun thinking of more things we could do.

I trained him the same way I trained him and Penny when they were 'puppies', by rewarding the right behaviour with treats. He didn't always understand what I wanted him to do, but I was patient with him and once he'd learnt something, he'd do it without being asked. When he heard the washing machine click at the end of its cycle, he'd trot off to empty it. Every time I went to get my shoes, Monty would appear: *Can I do that for you, Mum?* He'd always been a gentleman.

He changed overnight. Helping me had given him a new lease of life. He began to eat more and loved his walks again. Monty was back!

Golden retrievers are naturally helpful animals, so I'm sure he loved being active and useful. But I think it also took his mind off Penny and gave him a purpose after her death. It gave him confidence – he had some standing again. He and Penny had never been separated, so he'd been one of a pair his whole life. Now he was part of a twosome again, this time with me. He'd always been such a loving dog and this was the first time he realised that I needed him just as much as he needed me. I don't think he understood that before.

Having Monty help was changing me too. Boarding school had taught me to be independent – too independent, in some ways. At school, I felt like I was on my own because nobody else cared. None of the nurses or teachers would make a fuss of you. I got used to having to look after myself and, as my condition got worse, I hated having to rely on other people. It felt so unequal: when Peter helped me, It was as though I was doing all the taking. Whereas with Monty, I was caring too. I relied on him for help with everyday tasks, but he relied on me to feed and wash and groom him. He needed me as much as I needed him. To go from the one being cared for to the carer was a wonderful feeling.

My bond with Monty had always been superglue tight. From day one, he'd chosen me as his owner. Penny had chosen Peter – he's so kind and patient, I think she knew she'd get away with a lot more with him than with me! But now Monty and I were even closer. We were inseparable.

We discovered that he could balance me as I walk. With my skin, any kind of fall is disastrous, but holding on to Monty I felt much more stable. We got Monty a harness and he began to help me up and down stairs, and pull me up from the sofa. I relied on him more and more to get me through the day. I needed him. I was about to find out just how much.

I've had migraines since I was seventeen. The first time it happened I was on a bus coming home from work – my head hurt and my vision started to go patchy. Then I lost my sight altogether – it was an hour before it came back. The doctor said it was caused by stress.

The migraines came back every so often, and when they did I would always lose my sight. Sometimes I'd lose my language too. I'd try to speak and gobbledegook would come out. I could hear what I wanted to say in my head but my mouth brought out something different. It was very frightening.

When I was younger, it made me scared to go out by myself, particularly if I was on a horse. At first, I just rode near the horse's fields so that we wouldn't have too far to get back home if I lost my sight. But I got fed up with that, so I started going further out. If I got a migraine, as soon as my sight started to go, I would just let the reins loose and trust the horse to take me back to the fields.

But if you're out in the street without an animal and you lose your vision, it's terrifying. You can't see who's there to ask for help – or who might be a threat. I used to look at the people around me and try to memorise who was there and work out who would be a good person to ask for help, but it was too hard to keep it up. I went out on my own only very rarely.

One day, I was taking Monty out for a walk by myself and he wanted to go to the loo. I found a patch of grass for him to go on and then something strange happened. It looked like the grass was fizzing. I could see darts of light shooting out of it. I didn't understand what was happening. I put my arm out and realised I could see my hand but not my arm. Then I knew. A migraine was coming and I was losing my sight in patches. I tried ringing Peter, but by then I couldn't see the phone in my hand.

I tried not to panic. Very calmly, I said to Monty, 'Shall we go to the bus?' He started walking and I followed him, all the time thinking, *I hope he knows where he's going*. I had to trust Monty completely. He stopped and I stopped too. All I could do was pray he'd found the bus stop. Then I heard the bus pull in and I breathed a sigh of relief. Monty knew what he was doing.

I put my bus pass in Monty's mouth, as I normally do, and he gave it to the driver. But I must have looked strange because the driver asked, 'Are you all right, love?'

'No, I'm not,' I said. 'I've got a migraine and my eyesight's gone.'

'Don't worry, I know where you live. I'll let you know when we get there.'

I was grateful, but I was also getting curious. I wanted to see how much Monty could do on his own.

'Can you see if Monty knows where to get off by himself?' I asked.

I kept my faith in Monty and let him guide me to my usual seat on the bus. I sat down and waited. Then, as the bus slowed down, Monty stood up and I followed him.

The driver confirmed that Monty had got it right. Clever dog. Luckily the stop was just outside our house, so we didn't have far to go, but suddenly Monty just stopped dead. I guessed what had happened: the front gate was closed and he was waiting for me to unlock it. I didn't trust myself to open it without my sight – it would take my skin off my hands if I gauged it wrong. I asked Monty to bark. He did just as he was told and Peter came rushing out to the gate. He knew at once what had happened – he can always tell when I lose my sight. He said I was looking straight past him.

Monty had got us home. He'd seen I was in trouble and knew exactly what do. After that, I could go out by myself with total confidence.

The Christmas after Penny died, we were invited to a party. Peter and I were members of a social group for people with disabilities and we did all sorts of activities together: art, music, woodwork. The group was having a Christmas get-together in a restaurant, so I wouldn't be able to take Monty. I almost didn't go. By that time, we'd become a close-knit threesome and I didn't want to leave Monty behind. And whenever Monty couldn't go somewhere, Peter had to go back to being my carer: to help me with my jacket, hold my arm so I didn't fall, make sure I was OK all the time. It was awkward and it made us both feel self-conscious.

But we wanted to see our friends from the group and a neighbour kindly said she would look after Monty. Peter and I set off together, leaving him at home.

When we arrived at the party, the first thing I saw was a yellow Labrador. I thought of Monty: if only he could be here too. I wondered why this woman had been allowed to bring her dog inside, then I noticed the dog had a coloured jacket on and that he was helping his owner, who was in a wheelchair, in exactly the way Monty helped me. He took her jacket off for her and put the brakes on her wheelchair when she asked him to. I was curious, so I went up to the woman and asked her why her dog was wearing a coat.

'Oh, he's my assistance dog, Perry,' she said. I had never heard of assistance dogs before. She explained that Perry had been trained to help her day-to-day, just as Monty did for me. But unlike Monty, he was registered with a charity and had been given the coat to wear. It meant he could go to places pet dogs couldn't.

'He comes everywhere with me,' she said. 'He doesn't leave my side.'

'What, he can go anywhere? Shops and cafés? Hospitals?'

'Yes,' she said. 'I'm so much more independent now. Perry's changed my life.'

I watched her for the rest of the party. She looked so happy and relaxed with Perry working for her. He was looking after her and Peter was looking after me, but the difference couldn't have been clearer. They were doing exactly the same job, but she looked like she was having a wonderful time, and I wasn't, because all I could think about was how unfair it was on Peter. He couldn't relax and enjoy the party because he was always keeping an eye on me.

I knew then that I needed to get Monty a jacket so he could be my carer 24/7. Imagine if he could come to hospital with me, to sign language classes, to the shops . . . It would take so much pressure off Peter. I would be so much more free.

We arrived home and Monty was overjoyed to see us. He greeted me with my slippers and I hugged him. 'We're going to get you registered, Monty,' I said. 'You're going to be an official assistance dog and wear a jacket. Then we can go everywhere together.' I resolved to start searching the next day for a charity to help us. I told myself, I would not give up until Monty had his jacket.

chapter 10

From Rescue Dog to Assistance Dog

The next day, the search began. I sat down at my computer and put 'dogs helping people' into Google. I was amazed by the results. Under an umbrella organisation, Assistance Dogs UK, there are several charities all dedicated to training dogs to use their unique abilities to help humans. There were charities that helped people like me and the woman at the party, who had mobility difficulties. But there were also charities that trained 'hearing dogs', who let people with hearing difficulties know when the doorbell rings or the telephone goes, or more crucially, if a fire alarm goes off.

There are 'medical detection dogs', who look after people living with type 1 diabetes, as well as other life-threatening illnesses. The diabetic alert dogs are trained to let their owners know when their blood sugar gets too high or too low and fetch medical supplies. In training they are given breath samples and with their amazing sense of smell, they learn to recognise the change in odour associated with the change in blood sugar levels. There are dogs who help people with Addison's disease, postural tachycardia syndrome (PoTS) and narcolepsy, and dogs that can detect traces of nuts in food to accompany people with life-threatening nut allergies. Some nut allergies are so severe that even the smell of nuts can trigger it – there are dogs whose sense of smell is so strong that they can detect traces of nut in the air and warn their owners away from contaminated spaces.

The charity Medical Detection Dogs also trains dogs to detect cancer from urine or breath samples. With their exceptional sense of smell, dogs are trained to recognise the volatiles given off by cancer. The use of dogs in cancer diagnosis research may one day lead to diagnosing cancer in the very early stages, or to provide second screenings for cancers where other tests can be unreliable.

The charities' websites featured lots of personal stories from people who had dogs to help. Although all the dogs helped in very different ways, their owners often said the same things: the dog had given them more confidence, more freedom and independence, and a sense of companionship, all the things that Monty had given me.

I started ringing round the charities. I told them about Monty and asked if he could wear one of their jackets. The answer was always no. They all had intensive programmes run by expert trainers, which started when the dog was much younger. They only gave jackets to dogs who had been through their training programmes. And Monty was too old, they explained. He was nine and most assistance dogs will be coming up to retirement at that point.

Eventually I got to Canine Partners, an assistance dogs charity that helped anyone whose disability affected their everyday life or mobility. Its dogs were trained to do all the sorts of things that Monty did – opening and closing doors, pressing buttons, unloading the washing machine. I saw that they helped people with multiple sclerosis or spinal injuries. As far as I could see, they didn't help anyone with EB, but because of Monty I already knew that I would benefit from an assistance dog to help me.

By this point I'd almost give up on getting Monty a jacket. I didn't see how I could persuade anyone to take him on. But as I talked to all these people about the things Monty did, I could see more clearly the possibilities of having a dog to help me full time. I decided that if they wouldn't register Monty, I'd apply for an assistance dog of my own.

The lady I got through to at Canine Partners was very kind and helpful. She said they'd never helped someone with EB before, and she was worried about finding a dog that was gentle enough for my skin. I hadn't thought of that. I was lucky with Monty as he is an exceptionally gentle dog, and he'd never once hurt me. But the lady was keen to see if she could help.

'What sort of things would you need a dog to help with?' she asked.

'Well, actually, I've already got a dog who's helping me at the moment.'

'And what sort of things does he do?'

I read out the list of everything Monty did for me: balancing me when I walk, getting me up and down the stairs, picking things up for me, carrying things, undressing me, unloading the washing machine, undoing my splints and Velcro on my shoes.

'And who trained him to do all that?' she asked.

'I did,' I said.

There was a pause. 'You can't have done, surely! Our dogs are trained by experts and it takes years to train a dog to that level.'

'He's a very good dog,' I said. 'He's a registered PAT dog and he's well-behaved. He does everything I ask.'

'I still think it would be better for you to have a new dog,' she said. 'But when you come and see us, why not bring Monty along? We can see the sort of things he does and use him to assess the kind of dog you need.'

I put the phone down and my heart sank. I knew I should have been over the moon – I was one step closer to getting the kind of care I needed, that would make a real difference to my life and Peter's. But that was the moment it hit me: it wouldn't be Monty who would be my assistance dog. I'd seen how he'd thrived helping me and how much he loved coming out with me. I thought about how depressed he'd been when Penny died and was afraid he'd slip back into his old ways if he was left at home. Even if he didn't, I still felt sad at the thought of a new dog taking over.

I was so sad, I nearly didn't go to the assessment day. On the drive to Canine Partners HQ, I felt like a traitor. Monty was the dog I had grown to love and rely on and I couldn't bear the thought of leaving him at home while another dog worked for me.

When we arrived, I opened the car door for Monty. 'Stay,' I said, as I always did, and he waited in the car while I got my crutches out of the boot. Then I asked him to jump out and balance me. Peter, Monty and I went inside together.

Canine Partners HQ was amazing. I'd never seen anything like it. There were photos on the wall of dogs doing marvellous things and there were dogs being trained onsite by trainers in wheelchairs, learning skills to become loyal partners. I thought again, *But this won't be Monty*. I wanted to turn around and go home.

Then a woman called Nina Bonderenko introduced herself. Nina was the CEO of the charity at that time and she was lovely. I still feel so lucky to have met Nina that day. I could tell she was taken with Monty: she gave him a hug and made a big fuss of him and then we chatted about the various ways assistance dogs can help. They accompany their partners everywhere – into hospitals, shops and cafés. Everywhere I went, my new dog would be able to go with me. I thought again of Monty sitting at home alone while I took the new dog out with me. It was the last straw. I was about to get up and go home, and then Nina said, 'Show me what Monty can do. Let me see him helping you and then I can get an idea of what sort of dog you would need.'

So Monty helped me up and down stairs, picked things up when I pointed at them, and walked with me keeping my balance. I asked him to do everything that I had taught him to do at home and he performed perfectly. It was heartbreaking to watch. I feared he was sealing his own fate.

Nina was incredibly impressed.

'What a sweetie!' she said. 'He works so willingly – I can't fault him. He's a true gentleman.'

My heart broke. How could I tell her I had wasted her time? There was only one dog on earth I wanted to care for me.

Nina suggested we go and have lunch while she thought about our situation. We were very sombre over lunch. I asked Peter what he thought.

'We can probably cope with two dogs – there are two of us after all. Maybe I could stay with Monty while you went somewhere with the new dog.'

'Or we could just keep Monty and not worry about another dog,' I said.

'But you need a dog to take to college with you. And the shops. And hospitals.'

After lunch we still didn't know what we were going to do. Part of me just wanted to take Monty home and forget we'd ever been. But then Nina appeared with a huge smile on her face.

'I had a word with the trustees over lunchtime and they've agreed that if Monty's suitable, there's no point training another dog. Monty will be properly assessed both at HQ and at your house and in town, and if he passes our tests he can join the team. He'll be your Canine Partner.'

I couldn't believe it. All our problems would be solved. Monty was going to become my assistance dog. It was too perfect.

'I told the trustees that it was obvious you could rely on Monty,' Nina said. 'What you see is what you get with him. He's set in his lovely ways. This is who he is.'

I didn't know whether to laugh or cry. I hugged Monty hard and I couldn't thank Nina enough.

Nina told me that they had a lot of people asking if their dogs could be Canine Partners but they were never well trained enough and, up until now, they'd always said no. Monty was a one-off.

She told us she'd been watching us get out of the car when we arrived that morning, and seen how good Monty was when I opened the car door and told him to wait until I got my crutches out.

'Most dogs jump out of the car as soon as the door is

opened,' she said. 'When I saw Monty sit there so patiently, I thought, *This dog's different.*'

He was. I'd known he was special from the day that we rescued him. But to go from rescue dog to assistance dog . . . I never thought we would come this far.

chapter 11

My First Canine Partner

Monty still had to earn his jacket, of course. As I said goodbye to Nina, and thanked her over and over again, we agreed that I would return with Monty for extensive training so they could assess his behaviour in public places. Because of his experiences as a PAT dog, Nina wasn't worried about how he would behave around people or in hospitals, but she said that one of the major tests would be supermarkets. Monty would need to be trained to go near food without sniffing it or trying to eat it. I was willing to do anything; I didn't care how long it took to train him. All I wanted was to get Monty his jacket.

We were just driving out of the car park when Nina appeared again and stopped the car. She asked if we had time to take Monty into a local Budgens – they had a good relationship with them and they'd agreed to let us try Monty out in the supermarket, even though he was not yet officially a Canine Partner.

'Let's just see how he behaves when he's around a lot of food,' Nina said. 'Then we'll know how much training he'll need.'

Thinking that life couldn't get any more exciting, we parked the car again and followed Nina to the supermarket. I was hoping that Monty would behave well, though I had never put him in a situation that was quite so challenging before. I had already taught him to ignore food in elderly folks' homes and hospitals during his PAT work, and my 'no sniff' cue worked wonders at home. But the supermarket aisles were going to be much more tempting!

Monty was put in an 'in training' jacket – I felt a flicker of excitement at how smart he looked. We went into the shop together and Nina asked us to walk up and down the aisles while she watched Monty's behaviour. 'OK, Monty,' I said quietly. 'Do your best. This is important.'

OK, Mum.

We set off down the first aisle. 'Don't touch, Monty,' I said.

OK.

'No sniff, Monty.'

No problem.

Monty walked next to me, staring straight ahead, ignoring the food. I couldn't believe how wonderfully he was behaving. I walked him through roast chickens and fresh bread – I was sure that this would be too much for him and he would run over and sniff them, but unbelievably he stayed focused and kept on walking with me. He was good as gold. It was as if he knew what was at stake.

Nina was thrilled. She asked me to walk him again. I took him round the same route, up and down the aisles, and once again, he behaved perfectly. He did exactly as he was told and never sniffed once.

'Oh, he's a sweetie! An absolute sweetie!' Nina said. She decided then that she would send a trainer to come and visit us, as dogs can behave differently at home when they can relax and be themselves. But she said that if Monty behaved as well at home as he had done at HQ, then she saw no reason why he shouldn't be awarded a purple Canine Partners jacket.

No one has ever been as excited as I was. I think I could have flown to the moon without a rocket. Monty sensed he had done something special – he 'talked' on the way home, making little murmuring noises, just like Penny used to.

During the next few days I took Monty to as many new places as I was allowed. I needed to make sure he was confident in the role he was about to take on. I had absolute faith in Monty's abilities. But we had to make sure the Canine Partners trainer saw how wonderful he was too.

The day the trainer arrived dawned bright and sunny. She put Monty back in his 'in training' jacket, which would allow him to go into shops and cafés. Monty seemed taller; I'm sure he knew how lovely he looked. People stopped to admire him, but he took it all in his stride. We went into the local supermarket and my favourite café, and he behaved just as well as he had at Budgens.

We went back to the house and the trainer watched Monty run through all his jobs. She watched him unload the washing machine, open and close doors, help me up and down stairs and everything else he helped me with. He loved showing her all the things he could do. His tail wagged furiously the whole time.

At the end of the day, she said, 'He's been wonderful. He hasn't put a paw wrong. The jacket's his.'

I couldn't believe it.

'Nina said he behaved perfectly at HQ and he's behaved perfectly here. Monty's earned his jacket.'

To my utter delight, she took off the 'in training' jacket and replaced it with a proper fully fledged Canine Partners one. Monty looked so handsome. I could not have been happier. Canine Partners had decided that Monty deserved to wear their coat, and he never once let them down.

Monty becoming a Canine Partner changed my life all over again. Now he could come with me everywhere I went. Life became so much easier.

One of the biggest differences was people's reaction to an assistance dog. It was like parting the Red Sea when people saw Monty in his purple jacket; they stood

aside to let us pass. I used to worry about people treading on my feet or banging into me with bags, but not
any more.

At first, I didn't think I'd bother taking him to the
shops with me. Although he had been tested in the
supermarket, I couldn't see the point of taking him
there: I thought he'd just get bored. But a few days
after he got his jacket, a woman ran into the back of me
with her trolley. It took all the skin off my legs and feet
– I couldn't wear shoes for weeks. I realised just how
much protection having an assistance dog gave me.
'That's why I need Monty!' I said to Peter.

Everywhere we went, people noticed us and gave me
space. For someone with EB, the space is a gift. But
Canine Partners had warned me that the attention was
a double-edged sword. Monty became a celebrity –
everyone wanted to talk to him. All Canine Partner
jackets have a note on them asking people not to distract
the dogs when they're working, but not everyone
respects that. Peter and I tried an experiment: we took
Monty up the high street in Barnstaple without his coat
on and not one person spoke to him. We went back
exactly the same way, this time with the jacket on, and
every single person stopped. It took us three times as
long.

It was all quite overwhelming. At this point I was
still very shy and introverted, and I was meeting
hundreds of new people every time I went out. I
became good at spotting the people who were going
to approach Monty. 'Two aisles on the left,' I'd say to

Peter. 'He's going to come up to us, just you wait.' Sometimes they were crafty about it – they knew they'd been spotted and would disappear out of sight. Then, before you knew it, they'd be approaching from the other end of the aisle, and as they walked past they'd give Monty a surreptitious pat on the head.

Shopping becomes so much more difficult when someone is interfering with your dog. I knew they didn't mean any harm but it was unfair on Monty – he was concentrating on his job. If people asked me if they could say hello to him, I didn't mind. If he was busy, I just explained, and they understood.

But I was also starting to realise that I'd much rather get attention for having a dog than for being disabled. Part of the reason I was shy was that when I went out on my own, I could see people homing in on my hands, where the skin is badly scarred. 'Ooh, you've burnt your hands!' someone would say, and they'd tell me a cure for it. I'd get half an hour of cures for burns or psoriasis or eczema. I would get so embarrassed. And they'd often be talking quite loudly, telling you what was wrong with you, and everyone else would start to come over and look. But since I've had Monty, and then Teddy, no one's wanted to talk to me about my hands. They just want to talk about the dogs.

Another big change was taking Monty to hospital with me. One of our first appointments was at St Thomas' Hospital in London. I was worried about how he'd cope – he'd never been anywhere so busy before. At home, two tractors and four sheep was rush hour. But Monty never worried at all. He was born to shine. I think as long as I was with him, he knew he was safe. I was walking on air as I took him along the river and to the hospital.

The doctors and nurses loved Monty and he loved the attention. He sat quietly while I attended appointments and he helped undress me and take off my splints if the doctors needed to examine me. We stayed at Simon Lodge, a hotel next to the hospital for people who need treatment but don't need to be on a ward. The manager was a lovely lady called Janet, who sourced an electric fan for Monty in our room and made sure we had a room big enough for him to be with us. Monty was a star. He slept really well and never made a sound. Over the years he got to know his way around the hospital and grounds. He always took the same route to the station and back.

I found that I stopped worrying about my treatments at hospital. I felt it was my duty to make sure Monty had all he needed, and when I was thinking about him, there was no time to worry about me. As long as he was in the room with me, it took my mind off the pain. I felt I could put up with anything and not make a fuss. I didn't want to upset Monty, and that was my motivation to stay calm. It was like opening a door and letting sunshine into my life.

Being cared for by people can be difficult, but being

cared for by a dog is magic. And caring for Monty was an honour.

Monty had become a different dog. When Penny died, we realised how much she had looked after him. She had the stronger personality and he looked to her for everything: he let her eat first and always walked a little way behind her. Now Monty had a job; he wasn't Penny's sidekick any more. He was looking after me, thinking for me – and he knew how important that was.

At home, we started to play more games together. We used to say that Monty had a built-in clock: I fed him at 8 a.m. and 6 p.m. and if it was two minutes past his food time, he would come up to me, bow and run to the door. One day, I pretended to get up and he flew off to the kitchen. There was a pause while it dawned on him. *Oh, she's not here!* He came back, I started to stand up and he flew off again. Another pause. *You're not following me!* He did it five or six times in a row.

When he lay facing me, I would cross my arms and he would cross his paws. Then I would shake my head and he would shake his. He loved this game.

The more we went out, the more confident he became. When I took him into the town, we often went the same route, round to the bank and then back. One day, I wanted to go to the sewing shop, which was in a different direction and Monty just refused: *No, you can't go that way. I've turned round, you've got to go home.* He wouldn't budge. He had to go back the way he'd come.

He still had that amazing ability to draw people to him, people who were in pain or needed him. We were walking down a corridor in hospital when a surgeon came rushing out of one of the rooms. I suppose it must have been the operating theatre; he was still in his scrubs. He was crying. It was awful to watch. Then he dropped on his knees in front of Monty and started cuddling him. He stayed there for a few minutes with Monty in his arms, tears running down his face.

'I needed that,' he said. 'I really needed that.'

He got up and walked off. I was so happy that Monty was there. He could always provide comfort to those who needed him.

The skin on the inside of my throat was still very delicate. I suffer from terrible spasms where the muscles in my throat close up. It means that I can stop breathing at any time, even when I'm asleep. It is terrifying. We decided that someone should always be awake while I slept. We took it in turns to sleep and we each slept for two hours at a time. It was exhausting.

Peter was a 24/7 carer. He is good, patient and never complains, but naturally he got exhausted at times. Some days he was too tired to eat properly. One night I woke up, unable to breathe and Peter had fallen asleep by accident. I thought I was going to die. Monty sensed something was wrong and ran round the bed to pull the pillow from under Peter's head, waking him up. I was so grateful.

After that, Peter tried to be more careful and not let himself get so tired. We didn't think any more about Monty helping with my breathing. We thought it was a one-off.

chapter 12

A New Dog

It was 2006 and Monty was now eleven years old. All Canine Partners retire at twelve, and some stop work earlier. The dogs choose when they retire – if they stop doing what they're asked, you don't try to make them. They only do the tasks they're happy to do and, if they're choosing to do less and less, you start making arrangements for a new dog.

I could see this starting to happen with Monty. He was moving more slowly and he'd stopped jumping up for things. If I asked him to get something and he didn't, I didn't push him – I'd ask Peter to get it for me instead. It was obvious that he was slowing down.

At the same time, my condition was getting worse. I was having more and more hospital appointments and needed more and more help. By now, I was relying on Monty and I couldn't imagine what it would be like to go back to being cared for by Peter. Having Peter back as my husband and not my carer made such a difference. As awful as it was to think about Monty retiring, I had to start making plans for what I would do when he couldn't help me anymore.

I could apply for a new Canine Partner, but when I thought about having a new dog, I faced the same dilemma I had before. I just couldn't imagine how Monty would cope with being left at home while I went out with another dog or how he would feel about another dog taking over his tasks. Peter and I worried for ages. Eventually, I rang Canine Partners and asked for their advice. They said I ought to apply for my next assistance dog now. It could take years to find a suitable one.

I decided to stop asking Monty for help and to let him offer it when he wanted to. He was such a brave dog. He could still cope with undressing me and taking off my splints. He would still run to the washing machine to empty it. He loved picking up and carrying light objects, but I stopped him jumping up to open doors or pressing the pelican-crossing button.

Canine Partners invited us to HQ, where they would introduce me to some new dogs and see how I got on with them. On the drive there my heart felt heavy, exactly as it had the first time we went there. At least the first time, we'd always had the choice to go home and keep Monty. This time we knew that Monty would not be with us forever. I had to accept that I was beginning to lose him.

No one had told Monty that this was a sad time. He was so excited to be back at HQ. It is a wonderful place. Being part of Canine Partners is like being part of a family. We all call it the Purple Army. It is magical to watch the young dogs being trained. They have all sorts of training aids: special see-through washing machines, a fake shop, crossing buttons, beds and a lot more. The dogs all love the training. Some can hardly wait their turn – while the trainers are busy with other dogs, you can see how keen they are to go and join in. They only ever use dogs that are happy to help.

We were greeted by a Canine Partners trainer, Lucy, who explained how the day would go. They would try me out with several dogs and see how well we worked together. Monty would stay with Peter. I got up to go with Lucy and Monty tried to follow me. He couldn't understand why I was suddenly leaving him. I wanted to cry.

I was introduced to several dogs in turn. I was asked to walk with them, keep them to heel and give them treats to reward them for good behaviour while Lucy watched us working together. They were friendly, well-behaved dogs and they worked very nicely, but I found it difficult to get enthusiastic about any of them.

It was me that was the problem, not them. They were young, around eighteen months old, and it had been a long time since I'd been around dogs that age. They were lively and boisterous, and it made me nervous.

Lucy explained that this was one of the challenges the charity faced with helping people with EB. Assistance dogs have to be full-on: it's no good having a shrinking violet and expecting it to look after you when you're out. But an energetic dog could wreck my skin in an instant. When I'm around lively dogs, however well trained, I worry about my skin. I got anxious every time one of them took the treats out of my hand. I realised how lucky I had been with Monty. He was always so gentle.

I'd also had time to build up a relationship and connection with Monty. I couldn't imagine these new dogs as mine – it would be like being cared for by somebody else's dog, a dog you might meet on a walk. I just couldn't see how it was going to work.

We sat down to lunch in Canine Partners' canteen and I wondered what on earth we were going to do. But then the decision made itself. While we were eating, Lucy came and sat down opposite us.

'I've got good news,' she said. 'I've found a new home for Monty!'

'What? Monty doesn't need a new home!' I said. 'He lives with us.'

'But you're getting a new dog. You didn't think you were going to be able to have two dogs at the same time, did you?' she said.

It turned out that Canine Partners were always rehomed on retirement. They assumed that two dogs wouldn't work with each other – either they'd get jealous or worse, get lazy: both dogs would assume the other dog was going to do the job and no one would help at all. As she explained it, I saw that it was sensible: it was for the dogs' sake, to stop them getting upset and confused. But there was no way I could imagine Monty going to live with anyone else.

'I'm sorry, I can't do it,' I said. 'I can't give up Monty. He's mine.'

'Well, I'm afraid I don't see how you can have another dog then,' she said.

Rehoming Monty was not an option. I would never have gone if I'd thought that I'd have to give him up. I would have laid down my life for him and there was no way I was going to let him live with strangers. I had stuck by him from the beginning, when he was in a bad way and was impossible to train, and I would not part with him now. I told Canine Partners that I would get in touch with them if anything happened to Monty and we made our way home.

As Monty got older and less mobile, we began to rely more and more on my good friend Margaret. I'd met Margaret a few years earlier at the bus stop, when I'd been taking Monty for walk. She'd immediately fallen for him, stroking his fur and chatting to him. It turned out she lived nearby, so I suggested she come round for a coffee. We became friends and it was clear from the start that Monty adored her.

One very hot day I had a hospital appointment and, for the first time, I worried that Monty might not cope well with the outing. I didn't want him to get stressed, but I didn't want to leave him by himself either. Margaret very kindly said she would keep him for the day. I took him round in the morning before we left. I gave her his toys and some sausages to feed him if he got worried.

I was anxious all day. I hated the hospital and I hardly listened to the doctor. I felt raw. I couldn't wait to get home to Monty. When I arrived at Margaret's, he rushed out to meet me: his tail nearly knocked me over and he was 'talking'. Then he turned round and went straight back into Margaret's house. Peter and I started laughing. It was clear then that he loved me and Margaret equally. The relief was overwhelming.

It set a pattern. If I felt a day would be too much for Monty, he stayed with Margaret. We were even able to go on holiday without him. He had two devoted mums – we were so lucky to have found her. If I ever tried to ride my scooter past her door, he would sit down and wait for her to pop out and say hello or come for a walk with us. If anyone could have loved him as much as me, it would have been Margaret.

Monty was doing less and less for me, and sleeping more. I knew Monty would happily live with Margaret – by now he idolised her – but I still couldn't bear to part with him. I couldn't imagine not waking up to him pushing my slippers towards me and telling me to get up. I had no idea what to do.

After our visit to HQ, I sat down and wrote a long letter to Canine Partners. I explained that I couldn't part with Monty, but I badly needed another dog. I explained that I knew the problems with having two dogs together, and of finding a dog to cope with my skin. I didn't know if they could do anything to help me, but I wanted to explain in writing, just in case there was something someone could do. We didn't hear anything for a few weeks and we forgot about it. I accepted that I wasn't going to get another dog while Monty was still with us.

It was another very hot day. Peter was outside cutting the hedge, while Monty and I stayed inside keeping cool, with all the windows open. The phone rang. It was a man called Andy Cook, who told me he was the new CEO of Canine Partners.

'I've read your letter,' he said. 'And I see we've got a problem.' *Oh no, this is it*, I thought. I suddenly got very anxious. *A call from the CEO! What if they decide me and Monty are just too much trouble? What if they take Monty's jacket away from him?*

But Andy was incredibly kind and friendly. 'So you've still got Monty and you don't want to part with him,' he said, and we talked about how Monty was working less and less. We talked about finding me another dog.

'I think a new dog is always going be too boisterous for you, with your skin,' Andy said. 'The trustees just don't see how two dogs can work together, without putting Monty's nose out of joint. I don't think it's fair on the dogs.'

I agreed with everything he said. The situation looked hopeless.

'There's only one thing I can think of,' he said. 'We get you a puppy and you train it yourself, with our support.'

I couldn't believe it. A new puppy! Wow! Andy later said he could hear my jaw drop.

'If you have a dog right from the start, you can train him to be gentle with you. You find the litter, we'll test them to make sure they are suitable, and then the puppy can live with you while you attend classes once a week to learn how to train it. It's more likely Monty will accept it if you have the new dog from a young age. But if for whatever reason it doesn't work out, we'll take the puppy back and keep going till you find the right one.'

It was all sounding too perfect. I couldn't believe how well looked after I was. All the time I was thinking I would never have another Canine Partner, Andy was coming up with a solution.

'This is a first for us,' Andy said. 'If it works out, you'll be the first person to have two dogs at once and

the first person to train their own Canine Partner –
under our supervision, of course.'

He carried on talking, but I couldn't concentrate.
This was a dream come true. A new puppy and I could
choose the litter. I was so excited. I couldn't wait to tell
Peter. As soon as I put the phone down, I rushed outside
to find him. He was over the moon.

So this was to be the road we would all travel together.
Now we knew what direction to take. We just needed
to find the perfect puppy.

chapter 13

The Search

I knew at once that I wanted my puppy to be a golden retriever. It had to be. All sorts of breeds can be Canine Partners, though most are retriever breeds – they use Labradors, flatcoats, German shepherds and crosses of those breeds. They also use crosses with poodles: Labradoodles and golden doodles. But from the moment Aunty Gwen's dogs bounded into my grandmother's living room when I was a little girl, golden retrievers had been my passion. I couldn't imagine working with any other kind of dog.

Golden retrievers were originally hunting dogs, bred to retrieve game in the shooting field. Lord Tweedmouth developed the breed in the mid-nineteenth century, as a cross between yellow retrievers and water spaniels. Their background as a hunting dog makes them ideal assistance dogs as they love holding things in their mouths and are very gentle. They can carry an egg in their mouth without breaking it. I tried this on Heidi – I was in the kitchen and she was being particularly mischievous, so I put an egg in her mouth. She was astonished, but she didn't break it, just wandered around with it in her mouth, like a dummy. Monty was so gentle, it was easier for him to undress me without hurting my skin than it was for Peter. Golden retrievers are also friendly and eager to please and are easy to train.

But not all golden retrievers can be assistance dogs. It takes a very special dog to do this job. They need to be energetic, but also be able to calm down quickly. A lot of dogs could easily be trained to help but may not be able to relax when you need them to. Being fun and full of beans one moment, and calm and serious the next is a tall order for a lot of dogs. Getting it right is vital. There is no room for error.

Canine Partners don't have to come from pedigree stock – the charity has retrained one or two rescue dogs and Monty was the perfect assistance dog. But genes are a factor. Given how much you're asking of the dog, it helps to know as much about its family background as possible. And that will be much easier if you have a breeder who can trace their dog's line back through the generations.

When Robert was little, one of our rescue dogs, a Rhodesian ridgeback, chased him in the garden. The dog had previously been a guard dog, but no one had told us that. I was very upset and we had to rehome the dog. I wanted to get another one, but now I was going to be extra careful about where I got it from. I asked Aunty Gwen's advice.

'You'll have to get him a new dog quickly,' she said, 'otherwise he's going to be scared stiff of dogs his whole life. But you need to know it's going to be gentle. You want to get him one of Boss's puppies.'

She was talking about Fourwinds Bossanova of Lorinford, a pedigree golden retriever, whose descendants were still breeding. All her dogs had come from Bossanova's line, and so had Topper, my wedding present from Aunty Gwen, so that was how we ended up with Heidi.

They were remarkably gentle and good dogs. But we'd got Heidi over ten years ago, and although all breeders of pedigree dogs have a certificate showing the family tree, it goes back only five generations. It would be harder to track down Bossanova's progeny now.

So the hunt began for the perfect puppy. We made endless telephone calls and visited dog shows. We talked to exhibitors about our search and asked who they would recommend to breed a suitable puppy. When we met breeders, we explained what the dogs would be required to do, and they were honest with us and told us if a puppy from their line would not be suited to life as an assistance dog.

We knew that finding a litter could take years and that the kennel could be anywhere in the country. We might have to travel hundreds of miles to get our puppy. The litter might not even be planned yet. And even when we found a litter, it still had to be tested by Canine Partners and the chosen puppy would have to go through two years of intensive training before it qualified. Andy had warned us that not all dogs who embarked on the training ended up graduating as Canine Partners – some of them just weren't right for the job. And the dog also had to be able to work with my skin and with Monty. It was going to be a long road.

The more we talked to people about our search, the more we kept hearing one name: Colin Martin. Colin and his wife, Sheila, bred golden retrievers on Exmoor; their kennel was called Shannonstyle. They had had litters out of their bitch Crystal Maze (Tia) and a dog called Rosaceae Indian Prince Of Bridgefarm (Josh), who belonged to Maurice and Judy Shortman. Everyone said that the combined litters produced the most beautiful and sweet-natured puppies. Tia was a gentle girl with lots of personality and Josh was an adorable boy. It sounded very promising.

I met a couple on a walk with a beautiful golden retriever, a big dog with lots of lovely golden hair. His tail was beautiful and he walked like he knew how lovely he was. He greeted us like long lost friends. He was really bouncy but so gentle. We asked where they had found him. 'Oh, he's a Shannonstyle,' they said.

The more I heard, the more perfect Colin Martin's dogs sounded.

One morning, a woman passed by our gate with a beautiful golden retriever, who rushed over to play with Monty. We invited her in and she told us she was called Jo and the dog was called Barney. Monty and Barney played together and then settled nicely while Jo and I talked. All the time I couldn't stop looking at Barney. He was beautiful. Monty seemed really pleased to have company.

The boys lay side by side in the dappled shade. Their heads were touching. Every now and again they would wag their tails. I imagined they were swapping stories about their lives. Knowing golden retrievers, it would be stories involving food!

When Peter brought the coffee and cakes into the garden, they met him by the patio doors and formed a guard of honour to walk with him to the table. None of my golden retrievers had ever stolen food and these two were just as good. They lay down quietly again and I asked Jo how she met Barney.

'He's a Shannonstyle,' she said. 'I got him from Colin and Sheila Martin.' Peter and I nearly choked laughing. Jo didn't understand what was so funny, so we told her about our search for a puppy to become my next Canine Partner.

'If the puppy's anything like Barney, you can't go wrong,' she said. 'In fact, I think the Martins have a litter due soon.'

That was all the motivation I needed. I rang Colin Martin there and then. Yes, there was a litter due to Tia in a few weeks. I explained about the puppy growing up to become a Canine Partner and Colin asked lots of questions about it. What would his puppy be expected to do? How would it be trained? What would happen when it retired? I was struck by his obvious love of dogs – he really cared about his puppy's future. I was so pleased. I'm a firm believer that the way the puppy is treated when it is very young shapes its behaviour for the rest of its life. Even though we couldn't have been happier with Monty, I wanted a puppy from a loving home.

We chatted for ages and I told him Jo was here with Barney and what a lovely dog he was. Colin knew Jo and her late husband well. Colin had picked Barney out for Jo when she lost her husband. Barney was so lovely that I would happily have kept him if I could.

I told Colin about all the things Monty did for me. I explained how he happily helped me and how he always had time to play and be a normal dog. I told him that we lived very near Jo, by the beach. The puppy would grow up living close to them.

Jo got up to go home. As she got her things together, she said, 'Now, where did I leave Barney's lead?' As if on cue, Monty picked it up and gave it to her. We all laughed. When Jo left, we sat and talked about how much like Monty Barney was. I suddenly realised we had not asked who was in Barney's pedigree. It didn't matter. A kind nature was more important than anything else.

I was so excited but I tried to stay calm. The puppies

still had to be born, we had to meet them, and a trainer from Canine Partners would test them for suitability. There was still a lot standing between me and my perfect puppy.

Over the next few weeks we were like expectant parents. Every time the phone rang we rushed to see if there was any news about the puppies. The most amazing thing was that Colin and Sheila lived nearby, up high on Exmoor. We had always loved Exmoor – such a beautiful place. We thought that we might have to travel to find our puppy, and it turned out he was only a few miles away.

We tried to keep busy while we waited for the litter. We could see Monty slowing down but he still insisted on helping me. He would still push Peter out of the way if he went to help. Watching them compete to empty the washing machine always made me laugh.

During the previous six months my throat had become a lot worse. We had had several trips to hospital in London. They wanted to try to dilate my throat but I couldn't face it again. I could still remember how dreadful it was when I was twenty-one, after the accident with the curry. I kept being assured that modern techniques had improved the procedure, but I still couldn't face it.

I was also spending eight hours a day with splints on

my hand. I had been doing it for eighteen months now, and I found it so hard to do things one-handed. It meant I couldn't ride a bike. I was getting straighter hands but at a high cost.

Monty still loved helping me with my splints. He would even bring them to me to remind me to wear them. If I tried to hide them, he would soon find them. He undid my shoes with Velcro on – he enjoyed it so much, he would try and take them off no matter where I was! He was such a happy dog.

I had no worries about how he would get on with the puppy. He had lots of friends – golden retrievers attract friends, both human and canine. Even though he was getting older, he loved playing with dogs of all ages. One of his best friends was a little Jack Russell called Bill, they would meet on the beach and play chase. Bill was a tiny puppy when we first met him and Monty was very tolerant when Bill tried to jump up at him or chase his tail. He never once showed any signs of getting cross with him. If Bill got overexcited, Monty would simply keep turning his back on him until Bill calmed down. Once they had played, they would both sit happily while we all chatted.

Peter and I always took a flask of coffee to the beach. Monty knew the routine: play, then rest while we had a coffee break. It was just as well really because people would stop and chat to us. What should be an hour on the beach could easily stretch to two or more while we chatted to other dog owners. I would sit on my electric scooter, surrounded by dogs – heaven.

One morning, just as we were about to take Monty out, the phone rang. I nearly left it as we were all in our outdoor clothes, ready to go. Then I remembered: the puppies! I raced to the phone.

Sure enough, it was Colin. Ten puppies had just been born! Wow! Three girls and seven boys. Ten waggy tails. Colin told us that the bitches were spoken for, but that Canine Partners could have first pick of the boys in the litter for our puppy. I didn't mind: Canine Partners can be either sex, but I wanted a boy. Colin told us all about the litter, how long between each puppy, and what colours they were. It was agreed that we would wait until they were four weeks old before we saw them.

Never in the history of human life has four weeks gone so slowly. We started to prepare for our new arrival. Canine Partners sent me a file of puppy instructions. All puppy parents are given one, as well as Gwen Bailey's book, *The Perfect Puppy*. Gwen Bailey is an expert in animal behaviour and the book is her guide to training puppies. I was desperate to read it. I didn't want to neglect Monty, so I decided to read to him. He listened so intently and, sure enough, when we started training he was a great help. The book was amazing. I couldn't wait to start training.

We made sure we had everything in place for a puppy. Peter put netting under the five-bar gate so it couldn't escape. We installed a baby gate in the kitchen so we had a secure room for it. Monty had to get used to the baby gate – he'd always had free run of the bungalow until now. We thought he might be grateful to have a separate space for the puppy if it became too much. We still weren't sure how the dogs would cope together. All this preparation made me wonder what Monty and Penny had been like as puppies. Monty and I were so close now, it seemed strange not to know what his life had been like in his first few years.

Canine Partners had sent us a crate that would be a safe place for the new puppy to retreat to. We filled it with comfy bedding and put it in the kitchen and left the door open – Monty promptly climbed in it. He looked so content, we couldn't bear to move him. We shopped for toys, bowls and treats. Life was so exciting.

All Canine Partners need a toilet area in the garden. Peter had made an eight foot by eight foot area with bark chippings in it for Monty, and he enlarged it so that the new puppy could use it too. Toilet training Canine Partners is very important. They need to learn to go in specific areas. If their owners have mobility problems, they're not going to be able to pick up after them if the dogs go just anywhere.

I was still going to sign language classes. An extra incentive for learning to sign was that I often met people with hearing difficulties who had dogs to help, and I wanted to be able to communicate with them. The college had accepted Monty into the class. He loved the attention at coffee breaks. The classes were in silence, of course, and I began to wonder how we were going to cope with a puppy in the class with us, but our class-mates were excited to meet the puppy.

We phoned Colin and Sheila regularly to ask how the puppies were. The news was always good. They were growing well and getting active; I could hear puppy noises in the background when I rang. We made a date to meet them just before Christmas. I couldn't believe it. I was about to meet the dog who would be my 24-hour carer, my life-saver and my dear friend.

chapter 14

Enter Teddy

The day we went to meet the litter was wet and windy. We left Monty with Margaret – he wouldn't be allowed to meet the puppies until they were older. Colin and Sheila lived in a beautiful cottage on Exmoor, overlooking the sea. They told us that on a good day you can see as far as Wales. Today, we could barely make out the cottage through the mist.

I was so excited; I love puppies. I don't know what it is: the softness, that divine puppy smell. Colin had said there were ten of them, four weeks old. I couldn't believe that one of these dogs would become my carer, responsible for my life.

Colin and Sheila were lovely and gave us a warm welcome, which felt like a very good sign. Then they showed us into their kitchen to see the litter – another good sign. Some people breed in garages or outhouses, but these puppies were right in the heart of the house, in the warm, and would hear all the comforting noises of the family around them. They had put their dining-room table to one side to make room for a big pen filled with puppies.

There they were – ten little bundles of happiness, playing and squealing. 'Oh, they're beautiful!' I said, and as soon as I spoke, one little white puppy jumped up in the pen and ran over to me. He was pure white with large jet black eyes and a black nose – he looked like a seal pup. He started clawing my jacket, wanting to be picked up. I scooped him up and put him on my shoulder. He put his nose against my neck, burrowed under my hair and fell asleep. I said hello to the other puppies and stroked them, while the little white dog stayed snuggled up in my hair.

We visited the litter several times over the next two weeks, and every time the same thing happened. The little white puppy would hear my voice, his tail would start to wag, and he'd rush over. I'd pick him up and put him in the same place on my shoulder; he'd snuggle under my hair, and fall asleep. We started to call him 'Teddy Bear'.

It wasn't a good idea for me to build up a bond with any of them. There was still a chance that none of them would be suitable to be Canine Partners – they would be tested at six weeks' old and the tests were rigorous. They would take only the top two puppies, and if the little white puppy we were calling Teddy was not one of them, I would have to say goodbye to him.

But by now I had a connection with Teddy. It's hard to describe it but there was something there, something between us. I wanted so badly to keep him. I thought about offering to buy him as a pet if he failed the tests, but I also needed more and more help from a dog. If I bought him, I would have to live without a Canine Partner as I couldn't look after two puppies at once. I didn't tell Canine Partners about my relationship with him – he would have to pass the test fair and square. I began to dread the day that the litter would be tested.

When the day came, we drove back up to Exmoor to be there when the testing took place. Sarah Simpson, a trainer from Canine Partners, did some of the tests in front of us – dropping keys behind the puppies to see if they were easily startled and various other tasks, and writing down the scores in a little book. I was dying to know how well Teddy was doing, but I couldn't see what she was writing down. Then she took them all into another room, a few at time, to perform the other tests. She came back in and ignored the puppies while she added up the scores. My heart was in my mouth.

'Right,' she said. 'All of the puppies have passed.' That was a surprise – the tests are strict and it's unusual for an entire litter to pass.

'But two of them have done exceptionally well,' she said. 'The highest possible score is forty-five – this one's scored thirty-seven points and this one here got the full forty-five.' She scooped the two puppies up – a white one and a darker one – and held them in the air. I closed my eyes; I couldn't bear to look.

'These are the top two,' she said, 'and if I were you, I'd go with this one – he got full marks.' I opened my eyes. 'There's just something about this puppy,' she said, as she handed me Teddy.

I could see Colin and Sheila behind her, jumping up and down in delight – they knew how much Teddy meant to me. I held him close and he fell asleep under my hair. To this day, I don't know how he did it – a puppy scoring forty-five points is extremely rare. I think it was meant. I think he pulled out all the stops for me.

When we went to collect Teddy three weeks later, the day couldn't have been more different. The winter sun made everything glow and the view was bright and clear. As we drove, we could see the sea to our left; it was remarkably blue for January. Wild Exmoor ponies, with their thick woolly brown coats, grazed on the hill. It has to be one of the prettiest views.

This time, the puppies were old enough to see Monty. Monty had picked up on the excitement at home and bounced about more than usual. He seemed so well, I even worried that we had decided to retire him too early. I had told Peter that we could always train the puppy and then offer him back to HQ to help another person if Monty was still working well. But by now I was in love with two dogs equally.

We had no worries about how Monty would behave with the new puppy. He bounced out of the car and ran down the drive. We could hear the puppies barking, and Sheila came out to meet us and offered us coffee and cake. I felt like I'd landed in heaven. I couldn't believe this was happening to me. I was ten foot tall and grinning like a Cheshire cat.

Teddy was a picture of health and happiness – his coat was now a very pale cream, with the same thick dark markings round his eyes and nose. By now he was too heavy for me to pick up, so I sat on a chair and Peter put him on my knee. After he'd licked my face and tried to eat my hat he settled down, watching his brothers and sisters play with Monty. Monty loved being surrounded by bouncing puppies – it seemed to make him younger. Teddy jumped off and joined them, and when he got tired climbed back on my lap and fell asleep with his head under my hair.

When it was time to go, we put the dogs in the car: Monty with his seat harness on and then Teddy in his crate. He looked so tiny in it. I waved at Colin and Sheila as the car pulled away and knew we had made friends for life. There would be lots of visits to Exmoor to take Teddy back to see his first human mum and dad.

Teddy cried on the way home. He wouldn't stop barking, he was sick and made a mess in his crate. He did everything he could to protest. Monty put his head over the crate but it didn't do any good. We tried talking to him, but that didn't help either. It was heartbreaking to listen to. Finally, I put on a CD of our pastor Peter at church singing – silence. We knew the songs off by heart by the time we got home, but at least Teddy was happy.

We drove over Exmoor and down into Lynmouth, with incredible views again. I thought, *Such a beautiful place to be born*. It's amazing how lovely places look when your heart is up in the clouds.

Canine Partners had asked if I'd like to choose his name. They name their puppies alphabetically – all the puppies from the same year have names beginning with the same letter, in the order they were trained. In Teddy's year, the letter was 'E'. I was given two alternatives: Eno or Elvis.

I didn't know what to do. I certainly couldn't imagine shouting, 'Elvis' on the beach! But more importantly, to us, he was Teddy. I couldn't imagine calling him anything else. Even the postman knew he was going to be called Teddy. Canine Partners said they already had a dog called Teddy and they couldn't have two dogs with the same name.

I said I'd have to think about it and let them know. I had no idea what to do. It was only when we were driving in the car to Bristol for a hospital appointment that it dawned on me. 'Hang on,' I said to Peter. 'Teddy's short for Edward!' Peter's father, John Edward, had recently died and he'd been very close to our dogs – it seemed like a fitting tribute. I was so excited. I rang back and asked if we could name him Edward, and carry on calling him 'Teddy'. Canine Partners said we could. They call him Teddy Edward at HQ so they can tell him apart from the other Teddy.

Colin and Sheila registered him with the Kennel Club and were kind enough to ask me what I'd like his official name to be. The Kennel Club names are always wonderfully elaborate. We decided Ted's Kennel Club name would be Shannonstyle Edward Bear. His thirty-seven-points-scoring brother would be Shannonstyle Colin after his breeder – he would also be known as Eno, as Canine Partners were going to train him too.

Colin and Sheila gave me a copy of Teddy's family tree. I started to investigate and it turned out that his dad Josh's line could be traced back to Fourwinds Bossanova of Lorinford – the stud aunty Gwen's dogs had come from. I had got one of Boss's puppies after all. It must have been meant.

So now it was official: Teddy Edward was part of the family.

chapter 15

Teddy Comes Home

The first thing we did when we arrived home was show Teddy the toilet area Peter had made for him. He used it right away, which made us laugh. Then Monty decided he should go too!

We watched Teddy trot around the kitchen, getting used to his new surroundings. It was clear immediately that he had a very different personality from Monty. He was so much more self-assured. He had such a determined look on his face. 'Look at him!' I said to Peter. 'He's full of it!' And he was. Monty had grown up with hardship: he needed a lot of love and always wanted a cuddle. Teddy had grown up with love. As a result, he was full of confidence. I wondered if he might turn out to be a bit of a handful.

I prayed again that he and Monty would get on. Monty was such a calm, gentle dog and we'd landed him with a live-wire puppy. I hoped that Teddy wouldn't irritate Monty too much.

Monty was fascinated by Teddy. He watched him intently, as if he couldn't believe what he was seeing. *Look at him!* he seemed to be saying in astonishment. He turned and looked at me. *Look at this little thing! What's he doing?*

Monty and Teddy played together for a while, and then we could tell Teddy wanted to settle down. We took the crate into the bedroom, which was where Monty slept too. Teddy got into his crate and lay with his fur pressed up against one side of it. Monty lay outside the crate, but next to Teddy, with his fur pressed right up against the crate, pushing into Teddy's side. It was like they wanted to be as close as possible.

Canine Partners had supplied me with everything that Teddy would need when he arrived: his crate, lead, food, toys. We also had the folder full of advice and a list of numbers I could call if I needed help. I felt so well looked after, and I do to this day. If I ever have any problems, I only have to pick up the phone and Canine Partners will sort it out. When you have a puppy as a pet you can feel like you're on your own, with no one to ask for advice. With Canine Partners you're never on your own.

Sarah, who had tested the litter, had brought round Teddy's things. 'And here's his collar,' she said, handing it to me.

'But Sarah, it's pink!' I said. 'Teddy's a boy.'

'Exactly,' she said. 'Now when you go out with him, people are going to say, "Oh, is she a girl?" and you'll have to explain and that's going to get you talking.'

I thought I'd die. I was still shy and introverted – I hadn't got used to the number of people who came and talked to me when I was out with Monty. I couldn't imagine going out with a dog who had a pink collar as well as a jacket. Sarah knew me well. She knew having to talk to people would open up a whole new world to me.

While the dogs were sleeping, we made lunch. We had builders in our house at the time putting in new floors for us. They asked lots of questions about what Teddy would be trained to do and we told them all about Canine Partners and the ways Teddy would help us. They couldn't believe it was possible that a dog could do all that. All these years later, I still love telling everyone about all the things Teddy can do. I am so proud of him.

Teddy began to stir, so I lifted him out of his crate. His fur was so soft and lovely and warm. The perfect hot water bottle! He said hello to everyone. He didn't care about builders' bright yellow jackets or the noise the men made.

We had a sign language class that night. Looking back, I think we must have been mad to expect Teddy to come along to a class on the first night he was home. But I didn't want to miss it. After feeding him, we packed the car with all the things he would need. It reminded me of going out with the children when they were little. We brought a playpen to keep him in while we were in class, plastic sheeting to go on the floor and then newspaper to go over the top. We would be right next to him so we could make sure he didn't chew the plastic. Toys, towels, water bowls for both dogs – oh, and our homework! We packed the car like we were planning a military operation and set off for college.

You can imagine the welcome we got. Everyone was thrilled. Monty also got lots of attention. He behaved like a proud elder brother. We set up the pen, put water out for both boys, and said, 'You go to sleep now, Teddy, there's a good boy.' He played for five minutes and then amazingly did as he was told! Monty settled down in his usual place, next to the playpen so that Teddy could feel Monty's fur next to his, and they slept till tea break.

At break time I took Teddy and Monty out to 'perform' on the grass, then brought them both in for cuddles. It was wonderful. The boys were made so welcome. We passed Teddy round and told people he had to settle down nicely, so not to play roughly or excite him too much. We also reminded them that excited puppies usually wee on laps! College was never the same again. Teddy had arrived.

In the second half of the class, Teddy sat in his pen and watched us signing to each other. His little head went from side to side as he watched everyone move their hands. Then he went back to sleep. He was never any bother from then on in class. He even slept through my sign language exam. My classmates laughed and asked if I had written the answers on his lead! We were always the last to leave the building, except for the caretaker. All the items for Teddy had to be packed back into the car. Peter said we needed a trailer.

We took him to the toilet when we got home, fed him his last meal of the day and put his crate at the end of our bed. Monty helped me get ready for bed and Teddy watched his every move. It was as if he knew that one day he would be doing that job. Monty lay down beside Teddy's crate and fell asleep next to him.

Teddy woke once in the night with a whine. I took him out to the loo and he went straight back to sleep. He woke us at about 6 a.m. with another whine and I took him out again. Every hour on the hour, and after he had eaten, drunk, played or slept, I took him out to the loo. I gave him his cue to perform and rewarded him with a tiny amount of cooked chicken when he did. He was a fast learner. It didn't take him long to learn that if he went outside, squatted and pretended to wee, he would get his chicken. I became expert at watching to make sure he wasn't cheating! But the important thing was he was offering behaviour to get treats. This was going to be just what I needed when training began.

It was becoming clear that Teddy was a very lively puppy. The sign language class had been a bit of a red herring – luckily it coincided with the time when he would want to sleep so he'd been naturally quiet. In the day, he was most definitely awake. On his second day, we tried taking him to a café, but he wouldn't sit still – Peter had to hold him on his lap. I made a note that my first lesson would have to be settling him. But having Teddy on his lap made Peter very popular – when I went up to get the coffees, I looked back and saw that he was surrounded by women!

When we took Teddy out to the loo, he'd race round the garden. I realised then that a walk with me and Monty was not going to be enough – Peter was going to have to take him out for a proper run around. It was going to be my job to turn this fluffy little ball of energy into an assistance dog, who would come when he was called, stay when he was asked and be there for me 24/7, my life in his paws. As I watched him zoom round the garden, narrowly missing the trees, I wondered what I'd let myself in for. I hoped Sarah was ready for us.

chapter 16

Clicker Training

Normally, puppies selected as Canine Partners go to 'puppy parents', volunteers who train the puppies for the first twelve months of their lives, before going on to advanced training. Being a puppy parent is a very challenging job. Sleepless nights, puddles on the floor, chewed toys and training classes – and then the heartbreak when their puppy leaves them to train. But they are reunited at the puppy's graduation ceremony, and there's always the excitement of a new puppy to look forward to. Sometimes the dogs even go back to their puppy parents on retirement – the parents can't wait to have them back. Volunteers are vital to the success of the charity. Canine Partners opens doors to independence, but I always say puppy parents are the key to those doors.

In my case, we were doing things a little differently. I was going to be Teddy's puppy parent and his lifelong partner. Andy had told me that there were several other people in the same position as me, who needed a new Canine Partner but couldn't bear to give up their retiring dogs. They were counting on me to make it work. The pressure was immense.

Being there at the start of a puppy's life is a huge pressure in itself. Puppies are like little sponges, soaking up everything around them. How a puppy is treated in its early weeks is crucial – you can ruin a puppy in five minutes. If you tell them off or are cruel to them, they won't ever trust you again. Golden retrievers are very sensitive. With other breeds, you can shout at them and it's water off a duck's back, but golden retrievers are thin-skinned. Even now Ted is grown up, if I say, 'Come on!' a bit too briskly, he's hurt – you can see it in his face. With puppies, you have to be even more careful.

That was why I was pleased that Colin and Sheila Martin had been so loving. Sheila had made a point of handling each puppy five times a day, so they knew they were loved. All ten puppies – that's fifty cuddles a day! But I think it showed in their behaviour: they were all confident dogs, happy in their own skin.

Canine Partners trains dogs by reward, never by telling them off. That had always been my approach to animals too – I couldn't have worked any other way. I won't be cruel to anything and I just don't believe in force. With my EB I've felt like the underdog all my life, so the last thing I would want is for one of my dogs to actually be the underdog. And anyway, getting cross is not the most effective way. If you get cross with someone when they try to do something, they are not going to want to try again. But if you have given them lots of encouragement, they'll want to have another go. Dogs are just like people in that respect. Besides, it means the dogs are happy, and if they're happy they'll want to keep working. Even now, I say that Teddy never does anything wrong. If he doesn't do what I've asked, it's my fault for not being clear enough.

Canine Partners introduced me to clicker training, which I'd never heard of before. Sarah gave me a clicker – a little plastic box that makes a clicking sound when you press a button on its side. At first, I couldn't see the point of it – I'd trained Monty without one. But once I'd got the hang of it, it was like magic. What had taken me months with Monty took seconds with Teddy.

It works by getting the dog to associate the sound of a click with getting a treat. You can teach a dog this really easily: you just give them a nice piece of food or anything else they value highly, immediately after clicking. Very soon, they learn that they have to earn the click to get the treat, so the click becomes a reward in itself. But you have to treat them every time you click or the click loses its power.

The great advantage of the clicker is its accuracy: you can click at exactly the right point a dog does the thing you want it to. Your voice is not quick enough and it's also not consistent: the click is the same every time. Without the clicker, making the association between treats and behaviour is much harder.

I thought back to the early days with Monty and Penny, trying to get them to see the association between what they were doing and getting a treat. More often than not, they would see the treats in my hand and just go after them, and it was impossible to get them to do anything. If we'd had the clicker, it would have been so much quicker.

When the dogs have learnt to associate the sound of a click with a good behaviour, it becomes like a children's game, where you say 'warmer' if someone goes the right way, or 'cooler' if they go the wrong way. The click is 'warmer' and silence is 'cooler'. So, for example, if you want the dog to learn to use the washing machine, you give it a click and a treat any time he goes anywhere near the machine. Then he works out that the behaviour you want is something to do with the washing machine. So he goes up to it and you give him another click and a treat. You have to wait while he works out the click came from being close the machine and wait until he touches it. You click and treat when he does. Then you stop clicking so he knows that he needs to do more than just touch it. Each time you don't click and treat the previous behaviour, they have to work out what the next stage is.

When I was teaching Teddy the washing machine, this was the point he got frustrated: he started banging his nose against the machine. I had clicked that before but now I didn't. He knew I wanted him to do something with this thing in front of him, but he didn't know what he had to do to get more clicks. He got so cross, he nudged it, then he bit at it and, of course, I clicked and treated him. Then I stopped because although I needed him to bite it, he couldn't do it just anywhere: I needed him to bite the handle. By that point, he was pushing all over the front of the machine, so I clicked when he got near the handle. In the end, he was biting the handle and, suddenly, he opened it!

Clicker training takes a lot of patience, but it works. After enough time, the sequence becomes learnt behaviour. For Teddy, emptying the washing machine is like a person making a cup of tea: you fill the kettle, get the mugs out, put a teabag in without thinking about what you're doing.

The difficult part is learning how to use the clicker accurately. You have to click at exactly the right time, otherwise the dog won't know what action earned them the click. Young dogs move so fast that if you get it wrong, you can end up with a frustrated dog, who hasn't a clue what to do. To help get me started, Sarah got me to 'train' her. I had to decide what I wanted her to do and click when she got it right. It sounded simple, but I couldn't believe how difficult it was. It was a complete eye-opener. On my first go, I decided that I wanted her to switch on the light, but there are so many things in a room – I clicked her for going towards the door, but how could I tell her not to go through the door? We were in fits laughing. It was taking ages, but I kept trying and then bingo! Sarah turned the light on. Then Sarah dropped a tennis ball several times and I had to click at the exact second the ball hit the ground.

It paid dividends. By the time I came to train Teddy, I was much more confident with the clicker. Or so I thought!

At home, I was training him to pick up my hairbrush from the kitchen and bring it to me. When he went to pick it up, I clicked, but as I did, he turned his head and saw his tail. He thought that was why he had earned the click and started to chase his tail, round and round, only stopping to look at me, to see if he would get a treat. *Look, look, look! I'm doing it! Don't I get a treat?* I had to distract him and that was the lesson over for the day. He chased his tail on and off for two days until he realised there was not going to be a click.

chapter 17

Training Begins

My classes with Canine Partners started when Teddy was thirteen weeks old. For the first four weeks he was at home, I was training him on my own. Knowing what a ball of energy Teddy was, the first thing I had to do was teach him to settle down quietly. It's a huge challenge for a young puppy. I got a bowl of treats, a book and a clicker. I put Teddy on a three-foot lead, sat down with the lead under my foot and read my book. Immediately, he started prancing about and looking for attention. I ignored him. He chewed the lead, barked and whined. When he got tired, he lay down. I clicked and treated him, got up and played a game with him. That was the first lesson over. Every day, he had to stay still for a little bit longer before he got his click and his treat. After two weeks, he would lie quietly for thirty minutes. I was amazed.

We were still having work done on our floors and the house was in upheaval. It was not the right time to get a puppy at all! On the other hand, it meant I was confined to the conservatory or the kitchen – plenty of time to train. So that's what I did, on and off all day. Five minutes training, then play and sleep.

Canine Partners had given me a list of over a hundred tasks Teddy would have to learn before he graduated and said, 'See you in spring.' I thought they meant that he had to learn the whole lot before the spring, so I worked as hard as I could. Later when Canine Partners rang to see how we were doing, I found out that he wouldn't need to know most of them for another year. I think it stood me in good stead, though. When Teddy was older, I was grateful I had done so much with him in the early days.

The classes with Sarah took place in a pub, the Forest Inn, on Dartmoor. We met once a week for training sessions with Teddy's brother Eno and his puppy parent Sandra. Andy Cook told me later that they were training two dogs from the Shannonstyle litter in case mine and Teddy's relationship didn't work out. I felt so well looked after. Teddy and Eno were delighted to see each other again and they would play and wrestle after training sessions.

I have precious memories of classes in the Forest Inn. There was a roaring log fire and James and Irene, the owners, made us a pot of tea and biscuits after class and we would discuss what the dogs had learnt. Their dog, Spider, joined in the training sessions. Monty would sit with Peter while I trained Teddy, watching everything we did.

Sarah was a wonderful teacher. She had just the right amount of enthusiasm and drive. She was also a little bit strict – if she hadn't been, I wouldn't have achieved my goal. I learnt a lot from her. On the first day I asked Teddy to sit. He didn't do it, so I said it again. Sarah stopped me. 'Do you want your puppy to "sit" or do you want him to "sit sit"?' She said it was important for the puppy to learn the single word as the cue, otherwise next time you'd have to say it twice before he did it. You should say the word once and wait – and click and treat if he got it right. Training a puppy takes a lot of patience.

One of the first lessons in the pub was to teach the puppies not to eat food off the floor. Sarah put chicken and other tasty food in bowls on the pub floor. We took the dogs off their leads and let them loose. We stayed close to them and if they went towards the food, we would put our feet over the bowls. We weren't allowed to use our voices as otherwise when the dogs were older we'd find ourselves saying 'no' all the time. We wanted them to learn that there was no point trying to eat food off the floor as a foot would always cover it.

I was doing so well, until Sarah came over to talk to me. I tried to watch Teddy at the same time, but it felt rude not to look at her when she was talking and I turned towards her. In the seconds I had my eyes off him, Teddy went for a bowl. 'Watch your puppy!' Sarah said.

'But you were talking to me!' I said. She explained she had distracted me on purpose because that was what would happen when we were out – people would come up and talk to me and I needed to have my eyes on Teddy 24/7. I realised then that I had a lot to learn if I was going to succeed.

We taught him to do a 'loose lead walk' – any time he pulled on the lead, I stopped, told him to heel and lured him into a figure of eight. When he was in the right position, I clicked and treated him. It took a lot of patience, but he eventually learnt that we wouldn't move if he kept pulling.

When he was older, I taught him to pull so he could help me up from chairs and lead me upstairs – like Monty, we got him a harness that I can hold on to. I had to teach him just the right amount of pressure. The room I go to at the hospital in London is upstairs – Peter goes in the lift with our luggage, but I'm terrified of lifts, so I have to use the stairs. I used to hate it because I was afraid of falling over. Now, Teddy pulls me up the stairs so fast it makes me laugh.

Meanwhile, at home, I practised recall. If Teddy was inside, I stood outside and called for him, clicking when he came and giving him a high-value treat. I called him for his dinner and called him from room to room. He treated it as a game and loved it; everything we did was fun. Because he had no fear of being told off, he was a happy, confident puppy.

Gradually I let him run and play further and further away on walks. I called him back every time he went about twenty feet away from me. He got a treat when he came quickly back to me; too slow and no treat. He started to come back in shorter bursts without being called, which made me laugh – he would run a few feet away from me and come running back to see if I would give him a treat!

On the Tarka Trail in Instow in Devon, there's a point where lorries from the nearby marine camp cross the trail. I taught him to stop about twenty feet before he gets to the crossing – it amazes people when they see him run towards the crossing and suddenly turn around and come back to me. Even if he is running with other dogs he still comes back. All taught with a clicker.

Everything I was learning at the Forest Inn was coming in useful in day-to-day life with Teddy. One weekend we took Monty and Teddy to Sidmouth. It was raining when we woke up, but the forecast was good, so we decided to go ahead anyway. The weather brightened up as we drove.

When we got there, Peter walked Monty and I walked Teddy. We headed for the gardens on the cliffs. They are so beautiful – always a blaze of colour. As soon as we entered the gardens it started to rain. We didn't think we would be long, so we didn't bother going back to the car for our umbrellas.

The boys enjoyed a sniff and a stretch of their legs. Monty had been to the gardens when Penny was alive, but it was Teddy's first visit. By now it was pouring with rain, so we decided to take a shortcut back to the car.

Suddenly, Teddy stopped. I couldn't see what had caught his eye. He refused to move, in fact he turned round to go back the way we had come. I looked round the park to see what had spooked him and then I saw it. A huge jet-black statue of a fiddler, bending slightly. Teddy was terrified of it. He wouldn't go near it.

It's quite common for dogs to be frightened of statues. Before they attack, dogs stand completely still, so they are wary of anything that doesn't move. And they don't understand what it is: it looks like a person, but it isn't moving. I had already noticed that Teddy didn't like headless mannequins in shops. I could have taken him straight back to the car, but I didn't want us to go home on a bad note. I wanted him to have good memories of Sidmouth. I asked Peter if he wouldn't mind sitting under one of the shelters with Monty, out of the rain, while I tried something with Teddy.

I had my clicker in my pocket and treats in a bag. It was time to put my training into action. I didn't want to frighten Teddy but I also realised it was not good for him to walk away from something that worried him. I wanted him to understand that the statue was not going to hurt him.

I put myself between Teddy and the statue. He could still see it if he tried to look round me. Teddy and I walked back around the path away from the fiddler then walked towards it a few feet, and I clicked and treated him before turning away. I repeated this over and over, always keeping my body between Teddy and the statue, clicking and treating as I turned away. I was getting soaked. My hands were so wet I could hardly hold the clicker. We went diagonally across the park, in circles and straight across. We never went too close to the statue but Teddy was slowly getting used to it being there.

Now to test my theory, I turned and walked across the park with Teddy, but this time, I didn't put myself between him and it. We walked with him next to it so that he could see it. I clicked and treated him every time he looked at the statue. We slowly got closer, until he was able walk in a circle around it. I asked Peter if he could hold Teddy while I placed treats near the statue, about ten feet away from the base. Then I held Teddy's lead and I chatted to the fiddler. I laughed; I asked it how it was and pretended it was chatting back. Cautiously, Teddy stepped forward and ate the treats. I was thrilled. I got the treats closer and closer until he was eating from between the fiddlers' feet. I put treats in the fiddler's hands and let them drop near Teddy. He ate them up and wasn't worried at all.

Then I heard clapping. I turned to see a group of people in one of the shelters. They'd been watching us and they said they'd been convinced I would never get Teddy to go near it. They were thrilled to see how his confidence had grown.

Peter and I took the boys into the café to get warm. As we drank our tea, the rain stopped and the sun came out. I love Sidmouth in all weathers but in sunshine the red cliffs look amazing. On our way back to the car, I walked Teddy past the statue one more time. He didn't take a bit of notice of it. We went back three weeks later and he still wasn't fazed.

It had taken three quarters of an hour of walking round in circles, in the pouring rain, but I was on top of the world as we drove home. It was worth getting wet to give Teddy his confidence back. I had taught him to face his fears and win.

Peter and I loved every minute of the training. It was thrilling watching Teddy grow and learn. But it was hard work – classes once a week and homework from Sarah in between. And however much I enjoyed it, I still felt I had a lot to achieve. I couldn't help thinking about those other people who needed us to succeed so they could keep their dogs. I felt I had a responsibility to them.

Teddy was performing well, but he was still very, very lively. He was a quick learner – often too quick. He'd do everything he was told, but at top speed. And he always wanted to be one step ahead.

At the Forest Inn, we were teaching Teddy to tug gently so that he could help take off my jacket and socks. First he was taught to touch a tug rope, then he progressed to pulling it. Once he knew his cue really well, Sarah tied the rope to a closed door handle, showed Teddy a piece of ham, threw it through the door and closed it. 'How's he going to get it now?' I asked. Sarah said, 'Let go and give him his cue.' I let go of Teddy's lead and like lightning, he pulled the tug, opened the door and ate the ham. He'd done it before I could even say 'tug'. 'Oh,' Sarah said. 'Perhaps we can get him to wait till you ask him next time!'

But that was Teddy all over – he wouldn't wait to be asked. As soon as he knew what he was supposed to do, he just went and did it. It made him a very demanding puppy to train.

'You know, I don't know if Teddy's ever going to make it as a Canine Partner,' Sarah said to me one day. 'He's too full-on.'

As I watched Teddy wrestle Eno on the ground, I had to admit he was a bit over the top! But I adored him. There was no way I was going to give up. Teddy was going to become a Canine Partner if it was the last thing I did. I wanted him to succeed more than anything in the world.

chapter 18

Monty and Teddy

Any worries I had about how Monty and Teddy would get on quickly vanished. Teddy was still a real live wire, but when he was near Monty, he calmed down immediately. He never tried to play with him too much or annoy him or get in his way. He always let Monty eat and drink first. He just seemed to respect him. I told the vet how good Teddy had been with Monty and he was unsurprised. 'Well, Monty was here first, wasn't he?' the vet said. 'He's the boss.'

I looked at Peter and we burst out laughing. Monty was anything but bossy. We hadn't realised Monty was in charge – we thought Teddy was just being really good around him. But it seemed Teddy was bringing out a new side of Monty.

Monty was still slowing down, but Teddy's arrival seemed to have given him some of his *joie de vivre* back. Margaret was still a huge help – he was staying with her more and more. I was so grateful he had two loving homes. While Teddy was in training, Monty carried on helping me round the house. I asked the vet if we should stop him but he said Monty would stop when he was ready. I wondered again if we had got Teddy too early.

Then, when Teddy was just two months old, we realised that we'd got him just in time. We'd been out for a walk on the beach and had taken the boys home. Peter and I sat in the lounge chatting and Teddy headed off into the garden to tear around it like he usually did. Monty went to follow him, but he staggered and fell over. Peter tried to get him to stand but he wobbled badly. He couldn't walk. It looked like he was drunk. He kept trying to get up but he couldn't do it. It was awful to watch and Teddy was getting very distressed, so Peter cuddled Monty on the floor while I rang the vet. Teddy wanted to help Monty and kept trying to push Peter away.

We put a blanket round Monty and took him to the vet. I didn't know what was wrong with him, but it didn't look good. As soon as the vet saw Monty's eyelids flutter, he said he knew that Monty had had a stroke. The reason Monty couldn't walk was because his eyes couldn't focus.

My heart sank and I thought I was going to faint. Teddy leant against my legs. Monty couldn't leave us. Yes, we had Teddy, but we loved Monty beyond words. He was such a gentle dog. He didn't deserve to suffer.

We were given two options. We could put him to sleep or take him home and nurse him 24/7 and see if he would recover. The vet said it could take weeks of constant nursing, taking him to the toilet by supporting him on towels and hand-feeding him as he couldn't stand up. There was no doubt in our minds. I had never given up on Monty: not when we were told he was untrainable, not when we were told we would have to rehome him to get a new Canine Partner. We would nurse Monty for years if there was any chance of recovery.

Armed with medicine, we took him home. He and Teddy reversed roles almost instantly. Now it was Teddy's turn to lie gently against Monty to keep him warm. Within days, Teddy was fetching Monty's carry towel when he sensed Monty needed the toilet. We slept with not one, but two dogs between us on the bed. Peter carried Monty to his toilet in the night while I comforted Teddy.

We spent ages grooming Monty with a soft brush and rolling him over gently so he didn't get bedsores. I would take Teddy out for his walks, and Peter would stay with Monty. We never left Monty's side. When we got back, Teddy would find Monty a toy, and lie down beside him again.

Days drifted by. We went back and forth to the vet to check Monty wasn't in any pain. We began to settle into a routine, with Teddy watching him while we sorted out housework and food. The vet had told us that love is the most powerful medicine. More dogs recover from illness if they know their owners love and need them. Well, that was one medicine we had a ton of.

One day Peter and I were in the kitchen when Teddy came bounding in, barking. We ran into the lounge, fearing the worst. My heart was in my mouth. Was Teddy trying to tell us that this was it?

But instead Monty was up on his feet. He stood there, grinning and wagging his tail, back to his old self. He looked wonderful.

Both Monty and Teddy stood there wagging their tails. Patience had paid off. A visit to the vet confirmed that Monty had made a full recovery and was able to live a normal life. It was such a relief. Teddy found it hard to give up his role as Dr Ted and still brought us a towel when Monty wanted the toilet. To this day Teddy loves a towel. Offer him a toy or a towel and he prefers the towel. I think it reminds him of his best-ever pal.

Monty spent even more time with Margaret. They had a really strong bond. I would trust her with my life, so I had no worries about trusting her with Monty's. Having nearly lost him, we were more grateful than ever that Teddy would soon be taking over. It had been the right time to get him after all.

After Monty's stroke, their friendship went from strength to strength. There was a complete companion-ship between them, which I don't think I've seen so powerfully in dogs before. They were friends. People say that their dogs are friends but I've never seen such a bond between two dogs as there was between Monty and Teddy.

They mirrored each other. When Peter took Teddy out, he flew off and raced about. But if we were walking them together, Teddy would slow down and walk at Monty's pace, which for a young puppy is just amazing. And Monty came to admire Teddy. I think in the beginning he just saw Teddy as a puppy who needed looking after, but as he got older, he came to respect him too. Monty was always watching Teddy. He watched every move he made and Teddy never left his side.

They were so close you almost couldn't get between them. Monty and Penny would always cause mischief together, but Monty was too old for that now. He and Teddy played games together instead. Monty would get hold of a toy and squeak it. Teddy would immediately sit up. *Hang on! That's mine!* Then, he'd grab the other end and they'd pull each other round the room with it. They had great fun together.

One day it was snowing and Peter had flu, so I was on my own with them. I took them out to a field near our house. I'd taken just one tug toy with me, so I told them they had to share it. They took off across the snow, Monty carrying the toy. I watched them go. When they turned back towards me, I saw they were carrying the toy together, holding it between them in their mouths. They cantered back to me like circus ponies. Perfect teamwork. They looked wonderful. I never saw them do it again. I'd give anything to know what was going through their heads that day.

chapter 19

The Outside World

As the puppies grew older, our training classes started to prepare them for tasks they would do outside the home. One of the first things we taught them was how to behave at the supermarket. I was looking forward to having Teddy's help with the shopping. At the moment, Monty came with me to balance me and protect me from people knocking into me, but I would always get the shopping and pay for it myself. Canine Partners are trained to take things off the shelf, put them in your basket and give the purse to the cashier.

Sometimes at the checkout I found the cashier wouldn't want to touch my skin, so they dropped my change from a height or put it on the counter, which was worse because I couldn't pick it up. I'd walked out without my change so many times, ignoring shouts of, 'You've not taken your money with you!' I couldn't wait till I would have Teddy to help.

At the Forest Inn, Sarah made a makeshift checkout from pub tables and we took it in turns to be the cashier. At the supermarket, puppies have to move in a straight line so they don't get in the way of the trolleys – we lined up chairs close together and trained them to move between them. The puppies had to pick up shopping, put it in a basket and put it on the 'counter'. We also had to teach them to walk backwards, which is one of the hardest things to teach a dog. They have to keep just ahead of you when you're queuing, so they don't get rammed by the trolleys behind you or get distracted by other customers. But then they have to move back to give the checkout person your purse.

After practising in the Forest Inn, it was time to try Teddy in a real supermarket, Tesco in Newton Abbott. The first thing we were going to teach him was to pick something up from the shelf and give it to me. We chose a quiet aisle and Sarah suggested we start with something easy: make-up remover pads, as they're soft and on the bottom shelf. We asked Teddy to sit and I watched him carefully. When I was sure he was looking at the right thing, I said, 'Can you get that?' He started to move towards them. 'That's right – can you get those for me?' He grabbed the pads in his mouth and gave them to me – we were so astonished that he'd got it right first time that we all started clapping and cheering.

Oh, you like them? Well, that's easy! How many do you want? Teddy started pulling them off the shelves and wouldn't stop – we began laughing and a crowd gathered to watch. He loved the attention and started grabbing more. We had to buy them all as they'd been in his mouth – it took me ages to get through them. Teddy was still no less enthusiastic!

At six months old, I asked Canine Partners if I could attend a local puppy class to give Teddy more company. If he was going to be accompanying me round town, he would need to get on with other dogs. They agreed, and Puppy Gurus with Tracey Berridge at Barnstaple said we could join their classes. I would be training Teddy while Tracey was training her pupils. Tracey trains with rewards and clickers just like Canine Partners, so I knew we had the same ideas about training dogs.

All the other puppies were very good and their owners worked very hard to attain their certificates. The classes were great fun and Teddy fell in love with a beautiful little puppy, who he would play with every week. It was lovely to watch, but at one point they were playing so intently together we realised they'd forgotten we were there. Tracey told us to walk away and our puppies would get up and follow us. We tried that – they didn't! She suggested that I and the other puppy's owner go outside so they would wonder where we'd gone and come after us. No such luck. Eventually they got tired and came back to us, oblivious of all the fuss they had created.

It taught me a valuable lesson. Your dog's attention is momentary. If they get totally absorbed in something, no amount of calling gets their attention. Someone once called it 'going out of the door', when the dogs switch off to everything but what they are doing. It's great if you need a job done and don't want them distracted but not so good if you want to get their attention to do something else. I realised it was going to be vital to keep Teddy watching me. I couldn't let him get too immersed in something – I'd have to recall him every few minutes with tasty treats. I was about to start taking Ted to more and more places where there would be hundreds of things to look at and get interested in – I had to learn to keep his attention.

To prepare him for going outside, we also had to teach him not to be stolen. We put his lead on him and asked him to lie down in the supermarket. Obviously, Sarah or I couldn't pretend to steal him because he knew us, so we had to ask a stranger to help – we asked a young French student if he'd mind. We asked him to pick up the lead very gently, while I told Teddy to stay down. I clicked and gave him a treat when he stayed down and slowly, the man put more and more pressure on the lead, until he was almost trying to pull him. He pulled gently at the lead, while I kept saying, 'Stay down!' and clicking and treating Teddy. After that, if anyone touched the lead, he wouldn't move. *Sorry! Mum says I can't get up.*

Now, if anyone apart from me tries to take his lead, even Peter, he won't move. He will only go with Peter if I tell him to.

One of the biggest barriers to me going out by myself is the locks on toilet doors – my hands aren't mobile enough to use them. It sounds like a little thing but it makes a huge difference. I have a liquid diet, so loo stops are quite frequent. I can ask people to watch the door but it makes life much more difficult. If we go somewhere where there isn't a disabled loo, I'm stuck because Peter can't come to the ladies with me. And the amount of times I've asked a friend to help and then the door's opened and you see them on the other side of the room doing their make-up. They've just forgotten. It makes me so anxious thinking that someone could walk in at any moment. Monty would stand outside my toilet door, blocking the way, and it made such a difference. If I was with someone, I wouldn't have to ask them for help and I could go out by myself without worrying.

With Teddy, I took it one step further and I trained him to lie right up against the inside of the door. He was getting bigger by now and the weight of his body stopped anyone coming in. I had so much more freedom. Even if he did just that for me, he'd be worth his weight in gold.

Monty helped me a lot when I was training Teddy. He was still helping me around the house, so Teddy could watch and copy him. One day, I was training Teddy to pick up my keys and bring them to me but he kept dropping them just short of my hand. I found out from Sarah later that I'd been doing it wrong because I was reaching out for them – the minute you reach out for something, a dog will drop it. I should have waited for him to put them in my hand. But I didn't know that at the time, so I kept saying, 'Can you get the keys and put them in my hand, Teddy?' and he kept dropping them just in front of me. We'd gone through this routine about a dozen times before Monty got up, walked over, picked up the keys and put them in my hand. Then he turned around and looked at Teddy: *For goodness sake, just put them in her hand.* And then he lay back down again. I put the keys back on the floor and straight away, Teddy picked them up and put the keys right in my hand. *Oh, I see what you mean now!*

They worked really well together. When it came to Teddy taking over, I let Monty take the lead: he would decide when he wanted to stop doing something. When Peter took Teddy out to have a proper run around, I would use the time to let Monty do his tasks. I'd run through them and if there was anything he didn't seem to want to do, I would make sure to try and get Teddy to take over when he got back. Once Teddy had mastered something, Monty seemed quite happy to let him get on with it. But I would always let him have a go first.

We let Monty tell us when he wanted to give something up. One day, the washing machine finished its cycle and I waited for Monty to leap up at the sound of the door releasing, ready to start emptying it. Instead, Monty sat down and looked at Teddy. *I think it's time for you to start doing this now.* Teddy got up, took the washing out and Monty never did it again.

The first time we took Teddy to hospital was in an emergency. I was very ill and needed to see the specialists in London urgently. When we took Monty to St Thomas', we'd come out of the Tube and, instead of taking him straight there, we'd take him to a stretch of grass nearby to go to the toilet and then we'd walk round the long way to the hospital entrance by the river. This time, I needed to get there as quickly as possible. We came out of the Tube with Teddy and I tried to get him to turn left, so we could go straight there. He wouldn't do it; he wanted to turn right. 'Come on, Ted, we're in a hurry!' I said. But he was pulling the other way. In the end, I just followed him and he turned right, took me to the London Eye, through the patch of grass that Monty used to go to and then he found his way to the hospital, exactly the same route Monty took. I'll never know why he did that. He'd never been to London before – how did he know? Perhaps I instinctively wanted to go the usual way and there was something in my body language that was telling him to, but I don't think so. I was definitely asking him to go left. It was an emergency, I wasn't messing about. To this day, I can't work it out. Peter swears Monty gave Teddy a map.

When Teddy was ten months old, Monty had almost retired and Teddy had taken over. He hadn't officially graduated, but he had become responsible for most of my day-to-day care. Eno went off to advanced training when the boys were one year old and the once-a-week sessions in the Forest Inn came to an end. I carried on teaching Teddy new things, and Sarah would visit us and check on his progress and give us advice.

Teddy was still full of beans and totally over the top. Once, in the supermarket, I got the cue wrong: I gave Teddy the purse for the checkout and said, 'Jump up!' instead of 'Paws up!' Teddy never does anything by halves, so he jumped right up on the counter, waving his tail, and put his face right up against the checkout girl's, with the purse in his mouth. Luckily, she found it funny. Another time, I'd gone into the shop to get one or two things and I ended up getting more than I thought and my arms were full. I needed some bread, so I asked Teddy to get it and take it over to the check-out for me. The checkout in this shop was a bit higher than he was used to and he couldn't reach it. Teddy's trained to work things out; if he doesn't immediately know how to do something, he tries to find a way. He sat down, thought about it, turned his head and threw it at the checkout girl. It went hurtling through the air and she caught it. Teddy just sat there, grinning and looking pleased with himself for solving the problem. For a long time afterwards he was known in there as 'the dog that throws the bread'.

Teddy and I were working really well together and I began to appreciate his help more and more. The bond between us was getting stronger and stronger. But the most important lesson was to come. Teddy was going to learn to save my life.

chapter 20

Ted the Lifesaver

My throat was still bad and I was still having muscle spasms, which meant my throat could suddenly close up, even when I was asleep. Peter and I were still only sleeping for two hours at a time, so Peter could watch me while I was sleeping. Years of this had taken its toll and we were both shattered. It made daily life harder and meant we were less likely to go out and do things with friends.

When Teddy was about ten months old, he proved again just how valuable he was. Peter and I had had a busy day – we'd walked and shopped and tidied up, played with Monty and Teddy, and Peter had worked in the garden. We were both exhausted. I could hardly keep my eyes open, but I knew how tired Peter was. I told Peter to go to sleep and I would wake him in two hours.

Peter is a wonderful man. He never complained about having to stay awake or having to help with dressings. While Peter slept, I got into bed next to him and tried to read a book. I noticed I kept dozing off, but I didn't want to wake Peter. I knew how tired he was.

I decided to let myself doze for just a few minutes. A cat nap, or power nap, as they call them now. My throat was feeling fine. I stayed sitting up so that I wouldn't fall asleep too deeply.

But when I came to, I couldn't breathe. I tried and tried, but nothing happened. I had slipped down into the pillows and I couldn't move. Sleep paralysis is common, but for most people it wears off after a few seconds. For me, it can take a few minutes – it feels like hours at the time.

I could hear Peter snoring. Teddy and Monty were also asleep. I was petrified. *This is it*, I thought. *I'm going to die.*

Within seconds Teddy's head shot up. He looked at me and then rushed to Peter's side of the bed. He pulled Peter's pillow and barked to wake him up. Peter quickly turned me onto my side and helped me breathe again. The relief was intense. I couldn't believe Teddy had just saved my life.

The next day we talked about how amazing Teddy had been. We couldn't work out how he had known I'd stopped breathing. We had never trained him to do it.

'The bond between the two of you must have got so strong,' Peter said, 'he's picking up on everything you do. He just knew something wasn't right.'

But more importantly, we now knew that our old system – one of us staying awake while the other slept – was not safe. My throat was closing more and more. We didn't think we could rely on Teddy to wake Peter every time, but it was reassuring knowing he was there if something went wrong.

We told Canine Partners about how Teddy had saved my life and they suggested Teddy could be trained to use an emergency phone. Then, if it happened again and he had to wake Peter up, he could call an ambulance while Peter was helping me.

We had one fitted the next day. While the man was fixing the phone bracket to the wall, I trained Teddy to press the emergency button which would later ring through to a control room from where they would send out the ambulance. I asked Teddy to touch the button, and clicked and treated him when he got it right.

By the time the man had installed the phone, Teddy was pressing it as soon as I said 'touch button'. The man couldn't believe how quickly he had learnt. I took Teddy into the garden and he raced back to press the button as soon as I gave the cue. We were all deeply impressed.

After the lesson we took Teddy to the beach to relax him and let him meet his friends to play. It was already a lot more reassuring knowing that Teddy would be there in an emergency.

Weeks later we had another busy day. We should have slept during the day, but I hate sleeping in the daytime. I was really tired. Peter told me to sleep first as he was not too tired. But a few hours later I woke up not breathing and Peter had fallen asleep. So had Teddy. It was awful. My breath just would not come.

Teddy jumped out of his bed and rushed round to Peter and pushed his face with his nose. Peter shouted, 'Touch button!' and Teddy raced to the phone. I could hear the control room telling him the ambulance was on its way.

Peter got me breathing again and the paramedics came to check my oxygen levels. Teddy bounced about the room in excitement while everyone told him how clever he was.

We decided to take it one step further. Seconds are vital when you can't breathe. We decided that Teddy should press the button for the ambulance and then wake Peter, so the ambulance would be on its way while Peter woke and helped me. But I had no idea how I could train Teddy to call the ambulance without one of us giving him the cue.

By now, I was starting to think that we might be able to rely on Teddy to care for me during the night by himself. I'd already begun to rely on him in the daytime. If my throat closed during the day, he would immediately start barking until Peter came to help. I had no idea how, but it seemed he instinctively knew when I'd stopped breathing and that that meant my life was in danger. I had never trained him to do it – I'd never even imagined it would be possible. To this day, I still don't know how he does it.

I was worried that if I trained him to press a button when I stopped breathing at night, he wouldn't know what to do during the day. We decided that help at night was more important. I didn't stop breathing as often in the daytime.

Training began. I sat on a chair, with chicken and my clicker ready. I held my breath. Teddy wasn't fooled. He just stared at me. *OK*, I thought. *He's got to see that I'm really in trouble.*

I held my breath for longer, and sure enough he barked. I clicked and treated him. I tried again and just before he barked I said, 'Touch button.' He raced off to touch the phone. I had already told the control room I was going to train him, and they said they would talk to him, but not alert an ambulance. I assured them I would let them know when the training session was over.

Teddy soon understood what I wanted. Eventually, I stopped having to use the cue: I would just hold my breath and he would rush off to call for help. He thought it was a wonderful game.

It paid dividends. A few weeks later I stopped breathing in the night and Teddy called the ambulance and then woke Peter. Imagine how relieved we felt.

We knew then we could rely on Teddy to call for help. It meant Peter and I could sleep normally and we could relax, safe in the knowledge that Teddy had my life in his paws.

Years ago, I had been attacked – someone had grabbed my arms and it ruined the skin on my elbows for good. My skin can recover from damage to a certain degree, but once it is badly damaged, as my elbows were, it remains even weaker than the rest of my skin. Now I can't wear a coat or turn over in bed without bandaging my elbows to protect them from further damage, and I often have wounds there. One day, when the skin on my elbows was particularly bad, Peter had gone out and I decided to take the bandages off to let the air get at my wounds.

I took them off and tried to be careful not to bang my arms on anything. I went through to the bathroom and caught my arm on the door jam. I hit it at just the point there was no skin and it started to pour with blood. It really hurt. I had screamed as it tore the skin off further and the next thing I knew I could hear Teddy bark, then the phone emergency alarm going, calling an ambulance.

I was hurt but I didn't need an ambulance. I couldn't get to the bedroom to stop the alarm – I was bleeding so badly by now. I could hear the switchboard operator talking to Ted and I shouted to her that I was OK and that it was a false alarm. Thankfully, she heard me. I wrapped a towel round my arm and it wasn't long before Peter came home to help me dress the wounds again.

I called the emergency switchboard operator to explain. I told her that Ted had tried to bark to get Peter, but when Peter didn't appear he'd had to take matters into his own paws. He did the only thing he could think of to get help, which was to use the emergency button.

'I'd rather a hundred false alarms than miss the one when you need us,' she said. She laughed and added, 'Anyway, we love talking to Ted.'

We applied to Devon County Council for Teddy to be paid direct payments in recognition of the care he gives me. They were really understanding. I sent in details of everything Teddy did and what he needed, and they said they would decide if he qualified to be one of my carers. They had never paid a dog direct payments before, but it made complete sense now Teddy was responsible for my care twenty-four hours a day. I found out later that Teddy costs so much less than human carers, he saves the government over £56,000 a year.

We listed everything: his food, insurance, worm and flea treatment and all the rest. We wrote down all the things we usually bought Teddy. We were surprised at how much it came to, but Teddy is worth every penny we spend on him. Sometimes people in the street say to me, 'I bet that dog's expensive,' and it's true, he is. Canine Partners estimate that each dog costs £20,000 to train. But it's impossible to put a value on Teddy. To me, Teddy is priceless.

After a few weeks, to our delight, we received confirmation that he would be awarded direct payments. The wages helped, but what was more important was the recognition Teddy rightly received. I wanted the world to see how amazing he was.

We had to open a bank account for him, to keep the money separate from ours, and submit our receipts to the council every three months. We bought a file for the receipts and I made an appointment with the bank manager. When I told her I needed to open a bank account for my dog's wages she sounded surprised! I explained that Teddy was going to be paid for looking after me. In fact, Teddy was being paid to save my life.

The person I dealt with at the direct payments office said she would like to meet up and see what Teddy could do. We were taking Teddy to perform a demonstration at a disability awareness show in Exeter, so I suggested she come along and meet us there.

Teddy loves demonstrating. He just loves to be busy and, like all golden retrievers, he loves attention and showing off. He wowed the crowds with loading and unloading a washing machine and helped undress me. We showed him tidying up his toys and picking up dropped items. Teddy's tail wagged the whole time and I was thrilled to hear one of the audience comment on what a happy dog he is.

After Ted had performed, it was time to meet the lady from the council. Peter was manning Canine Partners' stall, giving out leaflets and selling pens and stuffed toys, so I went off with Teddy to the other side of the arenas. After saying hello to the lady, Teddy sat quietly while we talked. I explained the difference he made, not only to my life but to Peter's as well. I told her how Peter was a changed person. He had more energy; he was more relaxed and worried less about me. I told her how important it was that Teddy cared for me when we went out. Teddy would take my coat off, watch my toilet door and pick up anything I dropped. He could open and close doors and get help if I needed it. I explained that he helped me get home when I had migraines and lost my sight, just as Monty had. She was very impressed. I hoped it would help other assistance dog owners to receive direct payments in the future. I told her about Teddy's most important role: to press the emergency button on the telephone and then wake Peter.

At that point, I still didn't know what Teddy would do if my breathing stopped in the daytime and we weren't near the emergency phone. While the lady was writing notes, I started holding my breath. Teddy did nothing. I carried on holding it, putting my trust in him.

I was just beginning to think I would pass out when Teddy's head shot up. He looked from me to the lady who was still writing. He looked back at me and let out a very loud bark. I gasped for breath. Teddy thought I was still in trouble, so he barked again. I explained to the woman what I had done and she was amazed. I thought it would help her understand how vital Teddy is and how good he is at caring for me. I wanted her to know he really did listen to my breathing. I was also delighted that Teddy knew when to bark and when to press the emergency button: it was a huge relief.

Suddenly I heard Peter's voice behind me: 'Teddy, Teddy, it's OK. I'm here now. I'm here, Teddy. Good boy.' Peter came up to me, his face deathly white. He'd heard the first bark and asked someone to watch the stall. On Teddy's second bark, he was convinced it was an emergency and had run across the arenas, jumping over ropes to get to me. I was mortified. I'd had no idea he'd be able to hear Teddy where he was.

'Oh, Peter, I'm so sorry,' I said. 'I'm fine. I was just showing the lady what Teddy could do. I didn't think you'd hear.' I felt awful for worrying him, but at that moment, I realised just how safe I was. I have two wonderful, loving men looking after me.

And at least the lady from the council could see that both my carers were earning their wages.

chapter 21

Life with Ted

Teddy was still as lively as ever. But by now, it was one of the things we loved most about him. He was so enthusiastic about everything. He just loved working – we found we hardly ever had to ask him to do anything because he was already on his way. The minute he heard the washing machine click he was racing off to get it, shoving Peter out of the way if he tried to do it.

When Peter helped put my bandages on, Teddy would sit there watching him. *I know this is your job, not mine, but I'm still going to keep an eye on you.* And if he thought Peter was taking over one of his jobs – if Peter tried to help me take my coat off, say – Teddy wouldn't have it. He'd push Peter out of the way: *Hang on, that's my job!*

One of the major ways Ted helps me is getting me undressed. I can't wriggle out of things or they'll damage my skin and I don't have the strength to pull T-shirts off over my head in one go. Teddy is brilliant

– I just have to tap the back of my T-shirt and he'll pull the whole thing off over my head. It doesn't even touch my arms.

But I also have some very loose tops which are easy to take off myself. Once, I had one on and I was trying to get hold of it, when I felt Ted nudging my arm, quite insistently. *Excuse me! Excuse me! That's my job!* This top was actually quite nice material and I wasn't sure I wanted it going in Ted's mouth, but I gave in to him in the end.

People are amazed that Teddy can be gentle enough to undress me. Part of it is breeding – golden retrievers are bred to hold things very gently, but part of it is growing up around me. When he was tiny, he'd sometimes catch my skin accidentally. It was completely understandable – he was just a puppy after all, he didn't come ready made. But if he caught me, I'd say, 'Ow' and he'd immediately react: *Oh, I'm sorry, I didn't mean to hurt you.* And he'd try more gently next time.

He always worked so hard for me. Sometimes, he was too good. In training, the dogs are taught that some cues are non-negotiable. One of them is 'release' – if he's helping me up from a chair by pulling a harness, it's really important that he stops pulling at the right moment, when I'm on my feet. Another is 'stay'. 'Stay' has to mean 'stay – under no circumstances can you move'. Once, I was walking along the beach with a friend and I realised I couldn't see Teddy. I turned round and he was a hundred yards behind me, waiting. I'd said 'stay' because I'd seen another dog on the beach that I was worried about and I didn't want Teddy to go near him. I'd forgotten to say 'release' and poor Teddy was still there, waiting for his cue to move.

Another time, he was following me round the house, with a funny look on his face. 'What you doing, Ted?' I asked. He kept following me. *Mum, Mum!* I noticed he was drooling. 'What've you got in your mouth?' I said. He opened his mouth and he plonked a wet tissue in my hand. *Here you are, Mum!* I must have dropped it by accident and he'd carried it round the house, waiting to give it back to me.

No one can drop any litter around Teddy – he'll pick it up and give it to them. In the supermarket, a pack of jammy dodgers fell out of someone's basket and he went up to get them for him. 'No, Ted!' I had to call after him. 'You don't touch that. Not someone else's food.' They weren't going to want a packet of biscuits that had been in a dog's mouth. The next time I dropped something he looked at me as if to say, *Will you pick it up or shall I?*

One day, I'd been out with a friend and we got on the bus to go home together. It was a nice bus route, which took us right along the beach on the way home.

Teddy loves the beach. It's his favourite place in the world. It's all a big adventure to him. He jumps the waves and rolls in the sand when he's wet, and his coat changes to a lovely dark gold colour. He rushes around and plays with other dogs, but he always makes sure to come back to me every so often to check I'm OK.

The bus pulled into the stop by the beach and I was chatting away to my friend. It took us a while to realise the bus wasn't moving and everyone had gone quiet. It dawned on me that it was something to do with us. I had that awful feeling when you can't work out why everyone's looking at you, like your petticoat's showing.

'Look, do you want this stop or not?' the driver asked.

'I don't,' I said. 'I'm not getting off yet.'

'Well, your dog does! He just pressed the button.'

'Oh, Ted!' I said. I apologised to the driver, who was really quite cross, and he carried on driving.

'You cheeky monkey, Ted! We're not going to beach – we're going home!'

Ted was looking up at me with a grin on his face.

I took him home because I didn't want him to get his own way – I couldn't have him stopping the bus every time he wanted to play. But when we'd got home and put all our things away, I took him out again and we went back to the beach. If he'd wanted to go that much . . .

Ted was changing my life in all sorts of ways. I've always loved painting – I have happy memories as a child of watching a friend's father paint landscapes. I loved the magical way a picture could slowly appear on a canvas. I knew that one day I would try to paint too.

Like so many things in life, it wasn't going to be easy for me. I knew my throat would react badly to varnishes and turpentine, so oil painting was out. I tried water-colours but I could never master the technique. Then I found out about MAX paints, which you can use like oils, but are water-based. I was thrilled.

I booked in for art lessons. But I found the classes difficult. Peter had to come along as my carer – this was long before Monty had started to help. It was kind of him, but it drew attention to the fact I was disabled. The other people in the class treated me differently. In one particular class, I was down one end of the room and everyone else was down the other, talking about a Christmas party they were all going to that I hadn't been invited to. I can't stand being treated like that and it made me too self-conscious to paint. I was never relaxed enough to paint with my heart. I believe that you should lose a piece of yourself in a painting other-wise the work looks dead. For a picture to reach out to people, part of you needs to shine through.

I slowly stopped going to classes and I gave up the idea that I could paint. I put my paints and paper away along with my dreams of creating work I could be pleased with.

But now I had Teddy, things were different. He'd given me so much more confidence. People treated me differently when we were out – they stopped seeing me as a disabled woman and all they saw was Teddy. I could have been stark naked and they wouldn't take any notice. I called Teddy my invisibility cloak.

I decided I was going to enrol in art classes again. I told Peter that I wouldn't need him to come with me.

'What, you're going to go on your own?'

'Well, I'm not going on my own, am I? I'm going with Teddy!'

Once I'd booked the classes, I got worried. When the morning of the first class came, it felt like my first day at school. I packed my bag and unpacked it and packed it again. I took enough water for Teddy to bathe in, never mind drink. Peter laughed at me. 'They do have water in college, you know!' I just wanted to make sure I had everything Ted and I could possibly need.

I crept into the classroom. People were already there and they were quietly getting out their materials and making coffee. Peter helped me settle Teddy down with his bed under the table and his water. I got out my work. Peter left and I wanted to rush out after him.

The class started and we all had to introduce ourselves in turn. I said my name and then I introduced Ted. I explained that he helped me with all sorts of tasks, like opening and closing doors and taking off my coat. I saw everyone's face light up. A dog who could help you take your coat off! Then they all started asking questions. I happily answered them, not feeling self-conscious at all. I've always loved talking about Ted.

It was a completely differently experience. If I dropped my brush, Ted picked it up for me and he collected handouts for me from the teacher. Everyone was so impressed. They loved having him there. At break, they all wanted to talk to him.

I felt so alive and so happy. I loved painting again and I was so proud of Ted. The morning flew by and then Peter and I took him to the beach on the way home.

Teddy had been amazing. What a wonderful dog. I looked at him running loose on the beach with his friends and I felt like life was changing before my very eyes. Our adventure was just beginning.

chapter 22

Graduation

Even though Ted had been doing most things for me, he had not yet graduated as a Canine Partner: he still wore his 'in training' jacket when we went out and Sarah still came round to monitor his progress. All successful Canine Partners graduate after two years and we were doing everything by the book.

I wasn't worried about Ted's ability. Sarah knew what he could do – she'd been there he was trained and she came round to put him through his paces every so often. We'd run through all his normal tasks – taking him shopping, using the washing machine, opening and closing doors, his whole repertoire – and she'd watch him work and give me any advice she thought I needed.

Even after graduating, Canine Partners go through the same set of tests every six months. They're tested to make sure that they're happy and healthy, and that they can do still do all their tasks. The trainer also checks to see if there are any new tasks the partners need doing. And if the dog shows any signs of not wanting to work, at any age, they go into retirement. If Teddy decided he wanted to stop working for me tomorrow, that would be it – he'd never be forced. Not that you could force Teddy to do anything anyway!

Having been unsure about Teddy's chances at the beginning, Sarah was now very impressed with how well he was working. 'You know, I think your dog's going to be more famous than Lassie!' she said to me once.

Although Teddy had begun his life slightly differently from most Canine Partners, Andy Cook thought it was important that we go through the same system as all the other dogs, and I agreed. We did our public access test with Becca, another trainer from Canine Partners, who was lovely. She took Teddy into shops and cafés and watched his behaviour so she knew he was safe to go anywhere. Teddy passed with flying colours.

The next step was the two-week residential course that all Canine Partner owners go on before graduation, to prepare for life with their dogs. It was wonderful. It's the easiest place in the world to stay as everything is made for a disabled person. Everything raises and lowers: the sinks, the cookers, the work surfaces, the beds, so if you're in a wheelchair, you can have everything at the right height.

I learnt so much there – it was mind-blowing. I was like a sponge, trying to soak up all the information I could to make the most of my time there. I was exhausted when I got back! We went through first aid, healthcare, grooming, feeding, how your dog should behave in public, how much exercise and when. The best way to get your dog in a lift, how to put them in a car: all the things you never thought you'd need to know but of course you do.

They taught us how to pick up on dogs' body language. They brought a dog in the room and asked us questions about him: what does this dog like? What doesn't it like? Who does it like? Does it want anything? We had to get it spot on every time.

You also have to work your dog, to prove that they can do what you need them to do. I wanted to show Canine Partners that Teddy's behaviour wasn't a one-off – he could work well day after day. But suddenly I got nervous. That was when it hit home – that no one else was responsible for Teddy's behaviour but me. I couldn't blame the puppy parent – I *was* the puppy parent!

At one point on the course, the dogs are taken away from their owners and a trainer puts them through their paces to see how well they're working. Becca took Teddy off into another room and then she came straight back out again. 'He won't do anything!' she said. 'He won't do a thing I tell him!'

'Oh,' I said. 'How about if I try?'

All Canine Partners grow up taking instructions from their puppy parents, then their trainers and then their owners. But Teddy had only ever taken instructions from me. I took him into the back room and asked him to all do the things Becca wanted. He couldn't have been more obliging: *Oh, yes, Mummy, I'll do that for you! And what would like me to do now?*

He's just the same now: he won't do anything for anyone else. In fact, if someone else asks him to do something, I distract him or ask him to do something else. It's too confusing for him otherwise. Another dog owner we met on the beach tried to give him commands and got fed up. 'How come that dog only does what you tell him?' he said.

'Oh, I don't know,' I said. Secretly, I thought, *Well done, Ted!*

Teddy and I got through the residential course without a hitch and then we were ready to graduate. A ceremony was planned at Canine Partners HQ in Midhurst, West Sussex, for Teddy and five or six other dogs. It was a very proud moment. Monty and I had never formally graduated. Canine Partners kept offering to let us take part in a ceremony, but there was always a hospital appointment or I was unwell. To be honest, I think I was too shy. Even with Monty, I was still introverted. I couldn't face everyone looking at me. But training Teddy had given me so much confidence. I felt I had some standing again and I was just so proud of him. He'd changed me so much already.

When I'd been out with Becca on the public access test, I stopped and got chatting to an elderly man. He was on his own and looked really fed up and I wondered if he could do with someone to talk to. So I went over and said, 'Lovely day, isn't it?' He asked me all about Teddy and what he did and I told him.

As we walked away, Becca looked at me, impressed. 'You'll talk to anyone, won't you?' she said.

'That's all Ted,' I said. 'I wouldn't talk to anyone before.'

On the day of graduation, the weather was terrible. Everyone was asked to invite their family, the dog's puppy parent, its trainer and its breeder. But Colin Martin's car had broken down on the way in the bad weather, Sarah had been playing cricket the day before and smashed her knee, and my family were all at work. And I was the puppy parent! So on the day, it was just me, Peter and Teddy.

Eno, Teddy's brother, was also graduating. Eno had been partnered with a lovely lady whom he was helping with her mobility difficulties, and he'd been trained by a medical detection charity to alert her when her blood sugar is low. The charities often work together – for instance, if I lost my hearing, another charity could help train Teddy as a hearing dog.

Eno and Teddy hadn't seen each other since training and Teddy was thrilled. He could tell his brother was there before they'd even got out of the car – he was dashing about and trying to get out. When he saw Eno he was delighted, and we let them play in a paddock together before the ceremony started. We kept in touch with Eno's owner over the years and Teddy was always so happy to see his brother again.

For each dog graduating, Andy Cook, the CEO, made a speech. When it was Ted's turn, he told everyone the story of the unusual situation I'd been in, with Monty and my skin, and the story of how Teddy and I found each other. Then Becca spoke. She described me and Ted as a 'match made in heaven'. She talked about how well Ted performed on the course and said, 'There's a job here as a trainer any time you want it, Wendy!'

Then it was my turn. I had worried the whole time that I wouldn't be able to speak without crying. I had written two poems for Teddy's graduation: one from me, telling Teddy what he meant to me, and one from Teddy to me. Everyone at Canine Partners was encouraging me to read them.

In the end, I couldn't do it. I couldn't trust myself not to cry and who knows what damage it might have done to my throat. But I did manage to say a few words about Ted. I spoke about our perfect partnership. I told everyone how Teddy had pressed the button on the bus to get off at the beach and everyone laughed.

Andy explained why Colin and Sheila Martin and Sarah couldn't be there. 'So since Wendy is the puppy parent . . . This is the team!' he said, and pointed to me and Teddy. Everyone clapped. Teddy looked so proud.

I was always sad that I couldn't read the poems that day, although I think I was right not to risk crying. I'm so glad to have the chance to share them now.

To Edward Bear from Mum

I am not about to tell you what Teddy means to me –
I am going to tell Teddy.

You came into our lives like a tornado,
You were a non-stop gust of wind, never still.
Life was just a game.

You have made me laugh, you are a clown, never
   serious.

You have this inner beauty and calmness that
   others often don't see.
One minute you are chasing a Frisbee, the next
   your head is on my knee.

You have given me the ability to laugh at myself
   and accept who I am – and still you love me.
And I – well, I love you more than I can say.

With you I can fly, I can go out into the world not
   seeing or caring what people think of me.
If I am OK in your eyes, I am OK.

We have learnt a lot together, I have had more fun
    with you than I ever thought possible.

 I think you have enjoyed training me as well –
Sometimes I wonder who is training who!

After all –
I HOLD YOUR LEAD, YOU HOLD MY
    HEART

From Mum xxxx

The Perfect Partnership

Once upon a time . . . a lot of tail wags ago
On highest, deepest, greenest Exmoor, I was born.
Pure gold runs through my veins;
Even the sun is enhanced by my coat, I am
    golden.
On a wet and windy day in deepest winter, you
    chose me or did I choose you?
Was I made to care for you, or you for me?
You have taught me. I have taught you.
You watch me, I watch you.
You laugh, I dance, I sit, I roll over, open and close
    doors
And a hundred other things.
You feed, groom, protect, love and a hundred other
    things.
I rely on you, you rely on me.

Do I lead, do you follow?
Am I your shadow, or are you mine?
You hold my lead, I hold your heart
Embossed in gold.
In this wonderful, crazy, magical partnership we
   have pledged 'the perfect partnership'.
PS I have placed golden paw prints on your heart
   so as it beats, you know I am with you always –
TILL THE END OF TIME

From Edward Bear (Teddy)

chapter 23

Monty

When Teddy earned his Canine Partners jacket, Monty returned his. He was now fourteen. He still helped a little in the house, but he hadn't helped in cafés or shops or hospitals for a long time and now he was officially unable to. He had recovered so well from his stroke nearly two years earlier. Although he was slowing down and had let Teddy take over, he was still a wonderful dog and we treasured his company.

Then the unthinkable happened.

We noticed him snorting as if he wanted to clear his nose. He seemed fine otherwise – he raced Teddy to fetch my slippers or take off my socks as if nothing was wrong. He looked happy. But I wasn't. Deep in the back of my mind, a nasty memory was stirring.

Years ago a friend of ours had a golden retriever with cancer of the nose and I remembered the symptoms. I rang the vet and we took Monty in. As we sat in the waiting room, I felt as if cold water was being poured over my body. Teddy kept trying to lick Monty's face but I stopped him. I tried to keep positive. If I thought of a sunny day and birds singing, maybe I could will this not to be happening.

Monty snorted again in the waiting room and reality set in. It felt like icy fingers were gripping my heart. The vet confirmed my worst fears: Monty had cancer in one of his nostrils. He said it could be a slow-growing tumour and Monty could carry on for months – we had no way of knowing how much time we had left. But one thing was certain: our beautiful boy was dying.

We were given some medication to make him more comfortable and took him home. I couldn't believe it was happening, and like this. How could my happy, bouncy Monty be dying? How could life be so cruel? I rang Margaret, who was as upset as we were. Then we broke the news to our families. Peter's mum was devastated. She adored Monty. Somehow, it helped to know that others besides me and Peter were grieving for him. We felt less alone.

We tried to act normally and make the rest of Monty's life as happy as possible. He didn't know he was ill – he still acted the fool and tried to play. He wanted to run with Teddy but I kept him on a lead. If he ran about too much, he couldn't breathe.

In the end, it wasn't slow. We had several trips to the vets over the next two weeks and each time I feared the worst. Each time I thought Monty wouldn't come home. To our delight, he did.

But Teddy was never fooled by Monty's behaviour. He knew something was wrong and he was quiet around Monty. One morning, Peter and I were getting ready to go out and the boys were waiting in the hall to go for their morning walk. Teddy came into the living room very slowly, looked at me and lay down. I knew at once that something wasn't right. I went past him to the hall to see Monty. For the first and only time, Teddy didn't follow me to him.

He knew. He knew but I didn't. In some ways I'm now grateful for the oblivion I was in. Monty was having trouble breathing – it was clear it wasn't good but my heart and brain shut off the reality. We decided to take him to the vet again. Peter and I put both dogs in the car and we drove there in silence.

I told myself that we had had lots of trips to the vet and every time Monty had got medication and came home. This must be just a blip. As we arrived, I was already planning what we would do with the boys later that day. Monty got out of the car and I could hear his ragged breathing.

How is this happening? Monty had been his usual self that morning, getting my slippers and being silly. I had only left him alone for a moment before Teddy had come to fetch me, to tell me something was wrong. Surely he would be OK. The only thing nagging me was how dreadfully quiet Teddy was in the waiting room. He never moved a muscle. He lay with his head on his paws watching Monty. People said hello as they passed us and Teddy didn't even look at them.

I chatted to Monty in the waiting room to try and keep his spirits up – and mine. 'Everything will be fine, Monty,' I said. 'We'll see the vet and he'll give you something to help, and then we'll get home and we can go for our walk.' We would. We would be home just as soon as the vet had seen him.

But it didn't happen that way. The vet said that Monty couldn't breathe and there was nothing he could do to help him. He said he was sorry, but it was time to say goodbye. His voice sounded very far away, like I was listening to him from inside a deep black tunnel.

Teddy sensed I was upset and he began to get upset too. The vet said I should take Teddy out of the room as he shouldn't watch Monty be put to sleep.

My last picture of Monty is him lying on the table in the vet's surgery. He was trying to wag his tail even though he could hardly breathe. I really had thought he would be coming home with us.

I kissed his soft golden head and said I loved him.

I don't know how I got out of the door. I couldn't see for tears streaming down my face. I had always been there at the end for all of my dogs but I left Monty with Peter and the vet. I knew if I started crying, it would close my throat. Yes, I had had tears and upsets before, but if I opened the floodgates this time, I wouldn't stop. And I had to be strong for Teddy.

In my distress, I had put Teddy's lead on Monty and now didn't have one for Teddy. The receptionist gave me a piece of cord to attach to Teddy's collar. My hands weren't mobile enough to keep hold of it, so I wrapped it around my arm. If Teddy had pulled at all, it would have torn my skin off. But he knew there was something wrong. He stayed close to me and walked gently by my side, like a little lamb. He never pulled or even looked around.

I knew I had to get to a busy place to stop me howling out loud, so I took him to the supermarket. I walked up and down the aisles like a zombie. I could sense that Teddy was grieving too.

Peter came to find us later. His eyes were bright red and his face was a deathly white. He had taken Monty home and buried him, then came looking for me and Teddy.

I remembered what we'd been told when Penny died – that an animal should see a dead friend so they understood what had happened. It was too late again. When we got home, Teddy ran into the house. He looked in every room, just as Monty had done with Penny, and then stood in front of me. I tried to cuddle him, but he turned round and lay where Monty had last lain on their bed. Then he got up and fetched the towel we'd used to carry Monty. He put it on the bed with him and gave a long, low groan. It was awful to watch.

Our hearts were breaking and so was Teddy's.

chapter 24

Ted to the Rescue

The next few weeks were very hard for all of us. We all felt Monty's absence in the house. Teddy was heartbroken. Monty had looked after him from when he was a tiny puppy, shown him how to care for me, and become his closest friend. For weeks, Teddy went through the routine of searching the house for Monty and then lying in Monty's bed with the towel. It was terrible seeing him so low.

But just as Monty had his work to give him purpose after Penny died, so did Teddy. We had to look after each other and that helped us through. The only thing that could help us get over our grief for Monty was having Teddy and knowing we had to keep going for him. I don't know if I could have coped without him. Gradually, Ted started to get back to his usual ways. His sparkle returned. And as Teddy grew stronger, so did we. We were now more grateful than ever for Teddy.

By now, Ted was responsible for my life on a daily basis. If I ever stopped breathing, I knew I could count on him to raise the alarm. The more our bond grew, the more I relied on him. Teddy started to look after me in all sorts of different ways.

My aunty Gwen had always told me that whenever I stayed somewhere new, I should look for the fire escape. In an emergency, you get confused and frightened and it's easier to get out if you already know what the escape route is. I always took her advice, and whenever Peter and I went away we looked for the fire escape in the place we were staying before we did anything else. Eventually it occurred to me that it might be useful if Teddy learnt to find the fire escape as well.

Teddy has an amazing memory and sense of direction. He always knows how to find his way back to the car – if I need to get out of somewhere and I'm not sure of the quickest way, I just say, 'Treats in the car, Teddy,' and then follow his lead. It comes in useful if I'm somewhere large and busy like Ikea – I'm sure a lot of people would like to have Teddy with them when they go to Ikea!

Every time we stayed in a hotel, I would take Teddy from our room to the fire escape, click and treat him. As I treated him, I would say the words, 'Quick, get out!' We'd run through this a few times until he knew the cue: I just had to say 'Quick, get out!' and he'd go to the fire escape immediately. It became a routine every time we went away. As soon as we unpacked, we would teach Teddy where the fire escape was.

But we didn't know whether he would react the same way in an emergency. I was teaching him in daylight, when I was perfectly calm and there was no note of panic in my voice. He would need to find the way out when I was scared and possibly in the dark too.

On one of our visits to see family, Peter and I stayed overnight at a hotel near the M4. We did our usual routine with the fire escape, took Teddy for a walk and settled down for the night. We fell asleep but in the middle of the night, we were woken by a terrible noise. It was the fire alarm. I tried to stay calm. I clipped Teddy on his lead and said, 'Quick, get out!' Sensing my panic, Teddy rushed out of the door, down the corridor and straight to the fire escape. We struggled down the stairs and stood outside with the other guests and staff. It was pouring with rain.

It turned out that a fire in a kettle had set off the alarm – everyone was safe and no damage was done. What I hadn't bargained for was the fire alarm being faulty. It wouldn't stop and Teddy refused to go back in the building while the alarm was going on. We had to wait outside till they fixed it, which felt like years. We were very cold and wet by the time we were able to go back in.

But we were safe. We told the hotel staff what Teddy had done and they were so impressed. It made us feel so much better to know he could get us out if there was a fire and could one day save our lives. This time it was just an electrical fault in a kettle. Who knows what it could be next time.

In November 2010, Teddy was to prove yet again how good he was in a crisis. I had a series of appointments at St Thomas' in London. We had an hour or two between appointments, so decided to take Teddy out for a quick run to stretch his legs. I was in my mobility scooter and Teddy was by my side as Peter and I made our way along the South Bank.

On the other side of the river I noticed that there were rows of coaches all the way along the Embankment. I'd never seen them there before, but I didn't think anything of it. Teddy and I carried on, past the London Eye, Waterloo Bridge and the National Theatre, until we got to a little shop I know, where a lady sells cards and scarves. She loved Teddy, so we always went in and said hello.

We had a lovely chat with her until it was time for me to start heading back to the hospital. Then we stepped out onto the South Bank and were hit by a deafening noise. A sea of people was pouring out of the coaches, banging drums and shouting. They swarmed across Waterloo Bridge like ants. It was the student protest against tuition fees, and tens of thousands of people were marching. We had no idea it was going to be happening that day. The noise and the crowds were frightening. And I was frightened for Ted. I didn't want him to get scared or anxious.

It was also nearly time for my appointment and there were thousands of people between me and the hospital. The thought made me shiver. I turned to Peter and said, 'We're never going to make it past that lot.' There was no way I could go anywhere near a crowd like that with Teddy. I went back into the shop and asked the lady if there was another way to the hospital. I was starting to get anxious.

'I think I'm going to have to call you a taxi,' she said.

I gave Peter my scooter and got in the taxi with Teddy. I told Peter to try and make it back to the hospital, but not to go near the protest. I said that I'd call him when we'd got there to find out where he was.

Teddy and I got in the taxi and I asked the driver to find a way to St Thomas'. 'But whatever you do, don't go near the protest,' I said. 'If you have to take me out of London, take me out of London, but please don't go near the protest. I really don't want my dog to get upset.'

'Don't worry,' he said, 'I can get you in another way.'

We drove round and round the backstreets and I held tight on to Ted. He was still so calm and collected, but I was terrified that if we got too close to the noise, it would spook him. The driver pulled in near the back of the hospital. I'd never been that way before and I had no idea where I was.

'I'll drop you here, you know where you are, right?'

I was so shocked I said yes, even though I didn't. He was a kind man and he refused to charge me for the taxi. When I got out, I was totally disorientated and I could still hear the roars of the protesters. I knew they were close. I sat down on a bench and closed my eyes. *Just get your head together, you'll be all right*, I said to myself. But I needed to get to the hospital and find Peter.

In the end, I decided to put my faith in Ted. I decided to ask him to take me to Peter, and hope that he would take me to the hospital. I did wonder if he would take me back to the shop, but I hoped he wouldn't.

'Can you find Daddy, Ted?' I said.

Of course! He got up and I followed his lead. We went over a crossing and up a flight of concrete steps, across a car park and into one of the buildings. I had no idea where we were; I just had to hope that Ted did. He took me up another flight of stairs and suddenly there was Peter, coming along the corridor with the scooter. Amazingly, he'd found his way back. To this day, I still don't know how Ted knew where he was going.

I thought Ted would be shaken up, but he undressed me and got me ready for the doctor, as calm as anything. The doctor said he was lucky that he hadn't left the building at lunchtime: lots of the medical staff had got caught up in the protest and hadn't been able to come back. There were patients waiting for operations with no surgeons to perform them.

Later on, we left St Thomas' thinking that it was all over. Then we saw a group of protesters, and we backed away with Teddy. The protesters went up to the hospital. There was a little elderly lady standing just outside and they said were looking for the Conservative Party headquarters.

'Well, it's not here!' she said. 'You needn't think you're coming in here!'

We found out later they occupied the Conservative Party headquarters in Millbank. They'd set fire to it and smashed windows.

It had scared me. I was still scared that night and I didn't want to leave our room in Simon Lodge. But through it all, Teddy had stayed solid.

A few months later, we took Teddy on a train and the guard warned me that he was about to blow the whistle. 'Will your dog be all right with the noise?' he asked.

'Well, I should think so!' I said. 'He was fine all through the student protest in London!'

Teddy always seems to know if something is wrong, sometimes before I do. One day I had a routine appointment with my physiotherapist and I took Teddy along as usual. Halfway through the session he started licking my upper arm. This was very unusual for him. Whenever we had any kind of doctor's or hospital appointment, he would always lie quietly beside my chair and only get up when I was ready to leave. After a while, my physio began to get concerned. She knew that Teddy was trained to alert Peter when I wasn't well. If Peter wasn't with me, he would find someone else instead.

I asked Teddy to lie down. He did but after a few more minutes he got up and started to lick my arm again. The physio asked if I had any pain anywhere. I said I'd had a twinge in the night in my ribs but it had eased off when I got up. She suggested I should get it checked out in X-ray. I agreed, but I felt a bit silly when I had to explain to the doctors that I was in X-ray because my dog was licking my arm.

As it turned out, Teddy was right. The X-ray showed a virus starting in the ligaments between my ribs. They said I would have been in a lot of pain in a few days if it had not been found so quickly. I was prescribed antibiotics and we gave Teddy a Bonio for being so clever. Teddy, who'd cared so well for Monty during his stroke and in his last days, was now looking out for me. Dr Ted was back. But Teddy's biggest feat was to come.

It was a clear November day in 2011, a year after the student protest. Teddy and I were in the house and Peter was working in the garage. He was building an arbour for the garden – he knows how much I love flowers. We were planning to grow a clematis over it and maybe a rose.

I spent the morning training Teddy to take his own jacket off. Even after graduation, I still taught Teddy new things if I thought of something he could help me with. Canine Partners suggest that you teach your dog a new task every six months so they don't get bored. But Teddy picks things up so quickly I run out of things to teach him. In no time at all, he was able to reach round and pull the jacket over his head. This was very useful, as it's hard for me to bend down to do his jacket up and take it off. By this time, my gullet had shortened, allowing acid to flow into my throat when I leant over, which led to more damage from blistering. Anything I can teach Teddy to save me bending over is a bonus.

Halfway through the morning, Teddy and I took Peter his coffee and biscuits. At first, Peter didn't hear us come in, as the machine was so noisy. I tried to get his attention, but it was no good: he ignored us and carried on working. In the end I had to switch it off before he noticed we were there. He'd never hear us if there was an emergency, I thought fleetingly.

Teddy and I went back indoors. We did some more training and played games. I hid treats around the house to strengthen Teddy's ability to find things by smell. I worked on a few named items I had hidden around the house.

I started to get everything ready for lunch. Peter was having cheese sandwiches and I was having soup. After the time in 1993 when I'd choked and Peter had had to give up work, I was told that I shouldn't eat anything that wouldn't dissolve in water: if it got stuck in my throat and I couldn't then drink water to help it go down, I could easily choke. All my food is puréed and then goes through a sieve. I can manage a dunked biscuit or soft bread as they become a soggy mess when wet. It means a fairly bland diet but one I am used to.

Peter had left the cheese for his sandwiches out in slices on a plate in the fridge. I've always loved cheese and I find it so hard to resist. I just love the taste – the stronger, the better. After what had happened in 1993, I was determined not to make the same mistake. But it was so tempting.

I said to myself that I would just hold a piece in my mouth for a moment: I wouldn't chew or swallow it, but I would taste the flavour. I reached out and popped a bit in my mouth.

The next thing I knew was struggling to breathe. The instinct to swallow must have been too strong and the cheese had stuck firmly in my throat. I held on to the sink but I could feel my legs giving way. I couldn't call for help or talk to Teddy. It was terrifying.

I could feel myself losing consciousness. I thought I was going to die. I saw Teddy go towards the kitchen door. *He's going out to play*, I thought. I'm going to die and I won't even have Teddy with me.

The next minute Peter was thumping my back. It really hurt. We had taken a first aid course at college and luckily he remembered that you really have to thump as hard as you can to dislodge anything that is stuck. Suddenly, I felt the cheese shoot into my mouth and I spat it out. The pain in my throat was awful.

I knew I had blistered it terribly. But – thank goodness – I could breathe.

I was shaking from head to foot. Peter sat me down and gave me some iced water to sip.

'It's a good job you came back when you did,' I said, as soon as I could talk.

'Oh, I wasn't going to come back. Teddy came to get me. I was using the saw and I thought I heard barking. It didn't sound like Teddy. I switched off the saw, opened the garage door and saw Teddy outside leaping in the air. I knew it was urgent. He only barks like that when you need help.'

We both turned to look at Teddy. He had let himself out of the kitchen and conservatory, and gone down the drive to the garage. He had barked until Peter heard him over the din of the electric saw, and then he had rushed back to me, bringing Peter with him. He had saved my life.

In recognition for his bravery and quick thinking, the PDSA gave him an award for saving my life. I have never been so proud.

chapter 25

Life without Ted

Not long after he'd saved my life, Teddy came down with a stomach upset. He was being sick and was clearly not his usual self, so the vet said he'd have to rest for a few days. I couldn't stand seeing Teddy so low, but he had cared for me so beautifully through all my physical difficulties and I wasn't about to let him down now he was ill. I tried to get him as comfortable as possible. He still wanted to help, but I insisted he rest. I would just have to get used to living without Teddy for a few days. It didn't seem like a long time; after all, I'd lived that way for years.

But those few days felt like a lifetime. I couldn't believe how different it was without a dog to look after me. When you have care as good as Ted's, you get used to it very quickly and start to take things for granted. It was only when it was taken away from me that I realised just how lucky I was.

Going out by myself was frightening. I always used to walk around any holes or anything sticking up in the pavement to protect the skin on my feet. Teddy had picked this up from me and now he automatically walked round anything that could hurt my feet. All I had to do was follow him. When I went out without him I realised how much I'd relied on him. I had to relearn how to watch the pavement when I walked. I felt like I'd lost my spatial awareness – I didn't register where steps or kerbs were. With Teddy, I'd know if there was a kerb coming because I'd feel his body move up slightly.

I was terrified of someone bumping into me. I could easily lose the skin off my elbows just by someone pushing past me. Or on my feet, if I'm in a queue and someone steps back on you. I went into Marks and Spencer when it was busy and had to come straight back out again. I couldn't shop with all the people around me. I felt as if everyone had spikes coming out of them.

I realised how much Teddy balanced me – I became terrified of falling. I had to ask someone to hold on to me. Before Teddy, I used to hold on to Peter when we went out. 'I think it's so lovely that you and your husband still go out arm-in-arm after being married all these years,' a neighbour once said to me. She laughed when I told her it was because I was afraid to let go. While Teddy was ill I went out with a friend and clung on to her arm in the shops – I felt like I'd turned into a little old lady overnight.

I've never liked having to ask people for help.
Before Teddy, I would end up not asking when I
needed something and then getting frustrated because
I couldn't do things. But I knew Teddy loved helping
me – and he got treats anyway, so if I needed something it worked out as well for him as it did for me. He
would always nudge me during the day to see if there
was something he could do: *What do you want? What
shall I do now?* 'All right Teddy, go and get my slippers.'
OK then, Mum! And off he'd go to get them. I missed
that now.

I had an appointment at the hospital to check on
my throat. It was just a barium swallow. I've had
them done before, but this was the first time I'd been
to the hospital by myself for years. I felt pure dread
when I walked in. I'm ashamed to say, I went to
pieces. I was a nervous wreck. I realised how brave
Teddy made me. When Teddy was with me, the
nurses would chat to him and it would break the ice.
I can't sit in a waiting room with anyone with a cold
or a cough: if I catch it, I can't fight the infection and
I can't cough or sneeze without it blistering my
throat. So I sat in a room by myself. If Teddy had
been there, I could have talked to him, given him a
cuddle or larked about with him. Instead, I just sat
on my own, feeling like the room was closing in on
me.

Without Teddy I felt confined to the house. A little
thing, like him watching my toilet door, makes all the
difference. I just have so much more freedom. One of

the days without Teddy, we were having lunch at a pub and Peter called out across the bar, 'Do you need to go to the loo?' I was so cross! I did but I said no – there was no way I was going to go once he'd asked, like a child.

I felt vulnerable without Teddy. I found myself thinking back to the time when someone had grabbed my arms and damaged the skin on my elbows. One of the frightening things about having EB is not being able to defend yourself. If anyone turns on me, I haven't got a chance. If they've got a hold of me, I can't push them away or the skin will come right off. But having Teddy made me feel protected. He would never attack anyone, but I knew just having him near me kept me safe. I'd never walk out in the evenings by myself, but with Teddy I'd happily go anywhere.

But the biggest difference was the feeling of weightlessness Teddy gave me. It was amazing how quickly that went away. I began to feel self-conscious and introverted again. Instead of being outgoing and enjoying life, I suddenly went inside myself. Just worrying. It made me feel like lead. Having Teddy gives a sparkle to my day. Teddy is magic – and I'm the magician's assistant. Now the magic had gone.

Teddy was back to his normal self soon enough. It was wonderful to see his bounce returning. But in those few days I'd had a glimpse of what a life without Ted would be like and I'd learnt an important lesson. I realised just how much he did for me and how much I took for granted. It made me value him all the more, if that were possible.

chapter 26

Teddy in the Limelight

Meanwhile, Teddy's amazing life-saving skills had started attracting quite a bit of attention. A few years earlier, Canine Partners had rung to ask if I would be willing to be interviewed for a magazine. It was the first time anyone in the media had shown an interest in Ted and I was delighted. I wanted to shout to the world what a wonderful dog he is.

I spoke on the phone to a journalist called Jo Payton. I told her all about Teddy and how he helped look after me. I explained about EB and how gentle he was. A few days after the interview Jo emailed the article to me to see if she had remembered what I wanted her to share. I was amazed. Jo had been so sensitive. I felt she really understood the daily struggle I had and the pleasure Teddy had brought to my life. The article touched my heart. For the first time I could see Teddy as others saw him, and it made me realise just how incredible my beautiful bouncy boy

was. Teddy makes everything he does look so easy
and natural that I sometimes forget that pet dogs don't
do any of the things he does. I rang my aunty Gwen to
tell her Teddy was going to be in a magazine. She was
so pleased.

We all thought this would be a one-off, but over the
years Teddy's fame began to grow. So good was the
article by Jo Payton that other magazines and news-
papers wanted to write about him. He appeared in the
Daily Express, the *Daily Mail* and the *Sun*, and lots of
other publications. We bought a scrapbook for all his
cuttings.

A local journalist, Tony Gussin, wrote a story for the
North Devon Gazette about Teddy going to Crufts to show
off his talents. Not long after it was printed, a man
stopped us on the beach and asked for Teddy's 'pawto-
graph'. We put Teddy's paw in the water then stood
him on the newspaper right beside his photograph. It
did make us laugh.

Teddy started to appear on television too. *Spotlight*,
the BBC's regional news programme for the south-
west, wanted to do a feature on him. Hamish
Marshall, one of their presenters, came out to meet
Teddy and film him working. He was a lovely man
and a dog lover – perfect. We had a wonderful time
sharing all the things Teddy does for me, and Teddy
was a natural as he showed off for the camera. It
seemed to take ages and Teddy was filmed from all
angles, performing all his tasks. Nothing fazed him.
He unloaded the washing machine several times so

Hamish could get a perfect shot of him. Hamish asked if he could film Teddy outside. I took him to the postbox near the house. Then Hamish asked if Teddy could use the cash machine. I explained that I hadn't trained him to use it yet, but it was on my 'to do' list. 'Could we go to a cash machine and see what he does?' he asked.

I love a challenge. We drove Teddy to the local bank to use their cash machine. I inserted my bank card and jokingly said, 'Where's my card, Teddy? Can you get it?' Teddy knew what my card was: if I dropped it on the ground, he had already taught himself to flip it over with his paw so he could pick it up in his mouth. To my surprise Teddy jumped up, grabbed my card and put it in my hand. I couldn't believe it. Another task to tick off my list. When I turned round, there was a huge crowd of onlookers, all smiling at Teddy. Hamish apologised for holding them up but they all said they didn't mind. They were just enjoying watching Teddy using the machine.

One of Teddy's greatest privileges is to be the British Olympic medical team mascot. The medical team arrange all the care for the British athletes – not just the ones competing, but everyone at Championship level. They look after 1,400 athletes. In 2012, they were taking part in the Gold Challenge – a countrywide fundraising event linked to the Olympics, to improve health and encourage people to try more sports. The team took the Olympic Sport Challenge, where they tried ten Olympic sports, including trampolining and tae kwon-do. They chose Canine Partners as their charity and rang Andy Cook to ask if they could use one of the dogs as a mascot. The team was named by a man called Gary Tedder and they'd called themselves the Tedder Bear Hunters.

'Well,' Andy said, 'I think I have the perfect dog for you.'

When Andy called me to ask if Teddy would do it, I was thrilled.

We went along to Olympic HQ in Charlotte Street, London, where Canine Partners organised a demonstration of the work Canine Partners do by Doyle. Doyle is a wonderful labradoodle, trained to a high standard by Claire Anthony, a Canine Partner trainer. Doyle is a great ambassador for the charity. We were introduced to the team and Teddy had a huge fuss made of him.

Olympic HQ is a very exciting place to visit – they have all the Olympic torches on display in glass cases labelled with the year and country they were used in. How kind of the team to choose Canine Partners. What an honour to be part of it.

I still come down to London a lot for appointments at Guy's and St Thomas' hospitals, and we try to visit our friends at Olympic HQ while we are there – a wonderful lady called Janet Smith at the offices organises our visits to see them all. Teddy senses the excitement when we arrive and always brings something to show them. It is lovely to have something positive to look forward to on a trip to hospital.

chapter 27

Strength to Strength

Teddy was always surprising us. We have to go past the children's wing to get to my clinic at St Thomas' and we were always meeting children on the way. The children loved saying hello to Teddy. Sometimes I put a little teddy bear on his back, so it looked like the bear was riding him and it made them laugh. Parents would come up to me and ask if their child could stroke my dog because they were missing their own pet dog.

I remembered my days at boarding school without Sammy and I wanted to help them. I decided to apply for Teddy to become a Pets As Therapy dog, just as Monty and Penny had been. Ted was always very friendly and seemed to love saying hello to the children. He does love attention! But I wanted to be sure that he was happy to do it and that he was the right dog for the job. I would feel happier asking him to say hello to all the children if I knew that he was properly qualified.

We asked Canine Partners if we could apply and they agreed.

'He's got to be tested first, so you never know,' I said to Andy.

'He'll walk it,' Andy said.

I wish I'd been so sure. People assume that assistance dogs make good PAT dogs, but it takes an exceptional dog to do both. They're very different skills. A Canine Partner's main focus is on their owner. When you're out, they're your personal assistant. People are supposed to ignore them – of course, they don't always, but the dogs are trained not to interact with anyone but their partner. They are all good with people and other dogs, but it is not their main role.

A PAT dog has got to be people-friendly. It has to be happy to be cuddled and talked to and stroked. Teddy was a very friendly dog, but I wasn't sure if he would cope with doing both jobs.

We sent off the forms and a lovely lady rang to say she would be testing Teddy. PAT dogs have to be tested by someone they've never met before and in a place they'd never been to before, to prepare them for the kind of work they might do. We agreed to meet on a grassy area of a local car park at the top of a hill, where I'd never taken Teddy before.

When the day dawned, it was blowing a gale. The wind was blowing so hard, we could hardly stand up. It was perfect test conditions as wind often makes dogs agitated. Not Teddy! He lay quietly while we talked, and ignored the other dogs and people eating at the burger bar.

He walked nicely to heel and was patient while the woman handled him and looked in his mouth. As had happened with Monty and Penny, she made a noise behind him to see how he reacted. It's very important that PAT dogs do not take fright and panic if something is dropped behind them or near them. If it makes them jump, they have to recover quickly. With Monty and Penny, they used a metal tray but this time she dropped a tin with pebbles in. It was even louder and it made me jump! I'd failed again. Teddy just ignored it.

Then we had to wait for the results. They don't tell you right away – you have to wait for references and for the paperwork to be completed. The letter arrived just before Christmas and I was thrilled to hear that Teddy had passed. I rang Andy at HQ straight away. 'I always knew he'd do it,' he said. It was a very proud moment.

When we started visiting hospitals Teddy was a dream, as I knew he would be. He never got confused between the two roles because I would always tell him when it's OK to be stroked. Normally when we're out, he won't try to say hello to people and waits to be told he can. If people come up to us and ask if they can say hello to him, I'll say to him, 'Go say hello,' and he does. If I give the cue, he'll just get up and play with whoever's there. It's lovely to give him the chance to roll on his back, have his belly tickled and do what he likes. Just play.

Teddy also did a session with the charity Dogs Helping Kids. Tracey Berridge, who ran the Puppy Gurus classes that we went to when Teddy was a puppy, had set up the charity to give vulnerable children the chance to spend time with highly trained, well-behaved dogs who show them non-violent, friendly behaviour. Gwen Bailey, who wrote *The Perfect Puppy*, which was indispensable when I was training Ted, is a patron of the charity.

Tracey asked if I would take Teddy along to show the children what dogs can do to help people. It was a group of children who had difficulty fitting in mainstream school.

I took Teddy along and when we entered the room I was greeted by a group of well-behaved young people. I told them all about Teddy and they were spellbound. Tracey suggested we rig up a checkout and get Teddy to go through his shopping routine. She asked if the children would like to act as the shopkeepers. Teddy and I pretended to shop and took our items to the checkout where the youngsters could serve us. Teddy was good as gold and performed his routine perfectly.

I did wonder what all the fuss was about – the children had behaved so well. Tracey told me later that they had been very rowdy until I arrived and that session had been the best-behaved she'd ever seen them.

By now, Teddy and I were so close that he knew what I wanted before I did. One day, I was taking him out for his walk when it started pouring with rain: I was in my mobility scooter and he was running along beside me. I had a habit of putting my mobile phone on my scooter, in a little nook by the handles, but if you went over a bump, it could jump off. I was motoring along and Ted was trotting along beside me. The weather was filthy. It was cold and blowing a gale and all I wanted to do was go home. I heard a little sound, a kind of *doink doink*. I looked round but I couldn't see anything, so I didn't think anything of it and carried on. Then I realised Teddy wasn't with me. I turned round and he was right back there in the grass.

'Teddy, come here!' I shouted. He looked up at me and didn't move. 'Come here, we're going home!' I went a bit further along, but he was still lagging behind.

'Right, if you're going to do that, I'm clipping you on, Ted,' I said. 'I'm sorry, but you're going on the lead.' I went back to him and fastened on his lead and we made our way home, with him running alongside the scooter.

When I got home, Peter said, 'I just tried to phone you.'

'Oh, did you? I didn't hear it.'

'Where's your mobile?'

I looked down at the scooter. 'Oh no . . .'

I went back down the track with Teddy. All I had to do was let go of his lead and he raced 90mph back right down the track. He picked my mobile up and handed it back to me. *There you go, told you you'd lost it!* That taught me to listen to him.

The same thing happened at the checkout at Comet. I was about to pay, so I got my purse out and Teddy put it on the counter beside me. The checkout girl told me that her machine wasn't working and we'd have to go to the other position. So off we went, and all of a sudden, Teddy pulled the lead out of my hand, rushed back, grabbed my purse, then came over to where we stood and put it on the new checkout. He'd seen I'd left it behind. The people in Comet couldn't get over it. Teddy's a natural-born helper.

Teddy was going from strength to strength and it was a joy to have him in our lives. We decided to buy a caravan so we could go away during the oilseed rape season. Teddy loved it. We only had to touch the caravan key hanging up in the kitchen and he would rush to the door. He was always welcomed on the campsites, even if they didn't normally allow dogs on them.

It was a chance for Teddy to expand his skills. I love thinking of more tasks he can help us with. It makes life easier for us and it's more fun for Teddy.

Setting up the caravan and taking it down was a lot of work for Peter, and I wanted to help but I was limited in what I could manage. I decided Teddy and I could help between us. I would sit on a chair and support the water and waste carriers while Teddy pulled off the covers. We had great fun. Sometimes Teddy was so enthusiastic he nearly pulled me off the chair as he tugged at the covers.

I taught him to zip and unzip my sleeping bag. It meant I would disturb Peter less if I needed the bathroom in the night. I taught him to open the caravan cupboard doors and shut them for me.

It makes me sad when people refer to his help as work. Teddy gets bored very quickly and he's never happier than when he is busy. He bounces about with his tail wagging as soon as I ask him to help me. It's all one big game to Teddy. And I always make sure he has time every day to be silly and mess around. I sing 'Tea for Two' to him and then he knows that's his cue to go off duty, to be just an ordinary dog.

Ted always has time to play and be with his friends. His best friend is a dog called Toby, a Jack Russell – we call them Little and Large. We met Toby and his owner Jane when a group of us went out in the rain to search for a lost dog. Jane and I became instant friends and she has been a tower of strength to me over the years. One day, we were out on the Tarka Trail and we were hit by a dreadful storm. I was on my scooter and it was a long way back home.

I suggested Jane stand on the frame at the back of the scooter so we could get back quicker. We rode along together in the horizontal rain, with Ted and Toby bouncing along beside us. We were helpless with laughter and the dogs could sense our jollity. We now call the scooter the Double Decker. Ted and I often walk with Jane and Toby, and they curl up together in the same bed after walks.

Teddy's only ever known love and kindness. He is a very happy dog. Someone once said to me, 'If I come back as a dog, I hope I get a home as good as Teddy's.' It was one of the nicest things anyone's said to me.

chapter 28

A New Start

Life with Teddy was one big adventure and he was bringing us so much joy. But there was still one big obstacle to our happiness. My allergy to oilseed rape was becoming one of the greatest barriers to living a full life. It had become life-threatening and it confined me to the house during the oilseed rape season. If I had a hospital appointment, I'd have to rely on friends around the country to text and email me to let me know where they'd seen rape growing. Then Peter and I would have to map out safe routes to hospital appointments.

One of my hospitals is a 120-mile round trip, and my furthest is in London, which is 250 miles away. We've been known to cover 800 miles in a week, sometimes over 1,000 in a month. Keeping up with all the appointments is exhausting and the battle to find safe routes to get there was the last thing we needed. Going on holiday was like planning a military operation.

A friend suggested that we go to France. She often went on holiday there and she could recommend an area where rape isn't grown – they breed horses and most of the land is pasture rather than arable. Another advantage is that their season ends just as ours is beginning. If we arranged it carefully, we could avoid the oilseed rape season altogether.

Canine Partners agreed that Teddy could go on holiday abroad with us. We would take the caravan and stay at campsites – Teddy loved the caravan, so we knew he would be quite at home in France. We took him for his rabies vaccination and then waited until we had his blood results to make sure he had immunity. The blood test is not compulsory but Canine Partners are always very thorough. We found out where there would be English-speaking vets on our journey through France and I made sure there was one in the town we would be staying in.

We went for six weeks and had a wonderful time. We stayed at Domaine du Roc in Brittany, right next to a tree-lined canal with plenty of shade for me and Teddy. My skin can't be in the sun when it is bright, and Teddy doesn't like to get too hot. Teddy was a great attraction on the campsite and in the towns we visited. We found a beach for him nearby and he soon made lots of friends. We spent most of our time relaxing by the canal or visiting friends who lived near the campsite. Neither Peter nor I have very good French, but we did our best and were amazed at how friendly people were when we tried hard to be understood. I've never felt as relaxed anywhere as I did in France.

On hot days we went out early before it got too hot for Teddy, then spent all day in the cool under the trees. We sat by the canal or outside a café in the evenings. It was heaven. And best of all, it was the first year that I hadn't had to worry about the rape blistering my throat.

We began to wonder about moving there permanently. Peter visited local tourist offices and farmers to ask about areas free of oilseed rape. Rather than going back and forth between the two countries, it made sense to live where there wasn't any oilseed rape at all. We would cope better and I would be safer. Another great draw for us was that there was a hospital only 50 kilometres away that treated EB.

It would have been perfect were it not for the fact that Teddy wouldn't be able to move with us. However great my bond with Teddy was, we knew that he belonged to Canine Partners, not to me. I couldn't just take him out of the country, and it was out of the question to move away and leave him. I would sooner risk the oilseed rape in the UK than leave Teddy behind. He would have been distraught to go to a new home, but in all honesty it would probably be the last straw for me if I left him. It would break my heart. He has been with me 24/7 since he was nine weeks old. You realise how much your dog means to you when you would sooner risk your life than part with him.

We left France after saying goodbye to friends both old and new. When we got back to England, people remarked how well I looked, but it didn't last long. Coming back to the UK was draining. Our old worries returned: we knew we would need to keep leaving the country while the rape was in flower, but what if I was too ill to travel? Being in France had given us a taste of freedom from the constant worry. It made coming home much harder.

A few months after returning, I began to dread the next spring. I felt like I had lead in my shoes. I had been told the next blister in my throat would be very serious. The thought that there was an answer just out of reach was tantalising.

Peter suggested we talk to my EB nurse and see what she thought. DEBRA, the charity for EB, assigns a specialised nurse to you. They're the most valuable thing EB patients have. We try to do as much as we can for ourselves, but when it comes to something serious, you have an intermediary between you and the doctors, someone who understands your condition as well as you do. They come with you to appointments and are there to offer support when you need them. I was about thirty when the nurses were introduced and I can still remember how much more difficult it was before them. Back then there was no one to ask for help.

We've been very lucky with our nurses, every single one we've had has been so nice and caring. My nurse at the time was no exception – she was a lovely woman called Jenny. I poured my heart out to her. She wasn't surprised that we wanted to stop moving and find a permanent place where we could settle down. She said that we should talk to Canine Partners to see if there was anything they could do. She offered to write them a letter herself in support, explaining our situation.

It had never crossed our minds to ask Canine Partners if Teddy could move with us. I emailed Andy Cook the next day and we went to HQ in Sussex to see him. Andy is so good. He solves all our problems, so I felt sure he would do his best for us again.

Sure enough, he wanted to do everything he could for Teddy and for me. He'd got Jenny's letter and had been thinking it over. She had written that she thought I wouldn't survive without Teddy and that he wouldn't survive without me. That was when it hit me just how strong our bond was. Jenny had nothing to do with the world of assistance dogs, but even she could see what Teddy and I meant to each other.

We talked over how it would work if Teddy moved with us. There would have to be strict rules about where we could live and we would have to be assessed twice a year. Either a trainer could come and visit us twice a year, expenses willingly paid by us, or we could visit HQ once a year and have a trainer come to us for the next six-monthly visit. We would happily do either – our family was still in the UK and we could always include a visit to Canine Partners on our trips back to visit them, but we would also have enough room for visitors to come and stay. We wanted people to visit and share our many blessings. Andy said he would talk to the trustees at their next meeting.

The next day, Andy rang. 'Well, you were the first person to have two dogs together, the first person to be a puppy parent and a partner, and now it looks like you're going to be the first person to live abroad with a Canine Partner.'

We couldn't believe it. It was a dream come true. We went home and put our bungalow on the market – it sold very quickly. We sold all our possessions and began to prepare for the move. It was all so exciting. A new start.

We were due to leave in February 2014. In January, Ted and I were asked to go to Great Torrington Senior School to talk about EB. I had to go in four times, as they held four house assemblies. I was so nervous the first morning. I'm used to talking about Teddy but not about my condition. It's difficult to describe the effects of EB without shocking people. It affects every moment of every day. In fact it affects me even before I get up. If I forget my eye ointment at night, I can wake to my eyelids stuck to my eyeballs. It is excruciatingly painful.

An eyelash in your eye is bad enough. Tearing off skin is dreadful. It can mean days in a dark room with bandages to stop the eyelids moving and causing more damage. Putting on clothes and shoes can tear off skin. Brushing your teeth tears gums. Eating is a nightmare. I didn't know how much of this to say at the school assemblies.

It was a shock getting up before it got light to give Teddy his run before school started. After an early breakfast at 6 a.m. then a walk at 7.30, we set off for school. I needn't have worried. The staff were all very, very warm and friendly. I relaxed and I showed the assembly a DVD of the BBC *Spotlight* programme. The staff and children were spellbound. I told them that Teddy knows the difference between help and play. When his jacket is on, he is helping. Take it off and it's playtime. All the assemblies went really well.

On the last morning we took a toy for Teddy, and when the talk was over the teacher asked if any of the children wanted to stay behind and play with Ted. Several youngsters and teachers stayed behind and we took off Ted's jacket and gave him the toy. They all loved it. Ted ran around getting the children to play with his toy.

Some teachers asked if we could talk at other societies and groups. We readily agreed to do as much as we could before we left for France. It was an honour.

We visited Torrington Rotary Club where, after a lovely meal, we talked about EB. Talking to adults was completely different. I think the members were shocked at how EB affects me, but even more shocked when I explained that a lot of children live very painful, short lives, with hardly any skin that isn't blistered or red raw. Unable to get enough nourishment, they often die very young. Those who do survive are in constant pain. Changing dressings is distressing for the sufferer, but also for the parents who have to constantly burst blisters. Our blisters are not self-limiting, so they will cover the whole body if left to spread. I have been very lucky in many ways.

Teddy was due to appear on the BBC's *Animal Saints and Sinners*, a documentary about animals who do extraordinary things. I'm pleased to say Teddy was to be a saint! They were coming to film him just before we left for France. So much was happening all at once. But throughout this exciting time, something dreadful was lingering at the back of my mind.

I was finding it harder and harder to swallow and talk. Doing talks had taken it out of me – I hadn't wanted to let anyone down, so I tried to ignore it and not think about it. But the truth was my throat was getting worse.

The BBC filmed us the day before we moved to France. We had a lovely time with the film crew and I was so proud of Teddy. True to form, he did everything at a hundred miles an hour – he was too fast for them to film him and I had to encourage him to do things slowly. I was interviewed for the programme, and I realised then just how difficult talking had become. I wanted to give it my all, but by the time we finished, I was shattered.

By now it was even hard to swallow and to speak. I had my medical records translated into French and we hoped I could make an appointment with a doctor as soon as we got to France. I wanted to have confidence in the medical team there.

But within days of the moving, my throat was incredibly bad. I hadn't been able to get an appointment at the French hospital and I didn't want the first time I went there to be in an emergency, so we decided we'd have to return to see my specialist in London.

We came back from France – I was so ill my good friend Jane had to help me book the ferry. We called off the move until we knew more about my throat. Jane found us a bungalow to rent in North Devon and we decided to wait until we had seen the specialist in London. When we did, it was not good news. In fact, it was the news I had been dreading for a very long time.

chapter 29

An Impossible Dilemma

My specialist in London wanted to operate. My throat was getting smaller and smaller and it was now only five or six millimetres – a normal oesophagus is thirty. Only an operation could stop it closing.

Ever since my throat was dilated in 1970, after the dreadful night with the curry, doctors have said that one day I would need another operation. It was so awful that I swore that I would never have it done again. I did everything I could to avoid it. But now I had to face facts: my throat was closing and it could be fatal.

The operation was my worst fear. It was in the back of my head every time I swallowed or had trouble talking. I felt like it had been coming up behind me, like a big dark rock getting faster and faster and bigger and bigger, and I had to keep running in front of it, otherwise it would catch me. Now it was right behind me and it was very dark. It was all I thought about.

I told my doctor in London that I couldn't go through with it, even if it meant I might not survive. He assured me that medicine had come a long way since 1970 and it wouldn't be as painful. I still couldn't face it.

We went to see my specialist in Exeter, who told me that it was a difficult operation to perform on a normal throat let alone one with EB. It's a risky operation and could be fatal. I also have the added complication of my oesophagus spasms, the way my throat contracts when I stop breathing in the night or if I cry. Once I cried years ago and ended up spending ten days in hospital on a drip because my throat closed. My specialist said the operation disrupts the muscles in the throat and it could make the spasms a lot worse. He advised me to wait and cope as long as I could.

As my throat got worse and worse, I was finding it more and more difficult to eat, talk or breathe. I had to face it, if I carried on like this I would die. It was an impossible dilemma.

It was a very hard time. The move to France had been postponed indefinitely and we had sold everything we had. We had to buy everything new. Because we were in a rental house, there were so many things Teddy couldn't do for me: we couldn't put tugs on the doors for him to pull them open and he couldn't open the washing machine with his mouth because it wasn't ours. We couldn't even get an emergency button fitted, so we had to rely on Peter staying awake again at night.

By now I was struggling to swallow. I was eating only liquidised food and hospital prescription food. My energy levels were low and I found it difficult to sleep. I stopped breathing several times a night.

It was becoming difficult to talk. I stopped making phone calls and I attended speech therapy to learn to stretch my throat by silent giggling. It would never be enough to keep me alive but at least I felt like I was trying. I still had no idea what to do.

Although I had said I would rather die than try the operation, I hadn't counted on having a dog like Ted, who needed me as much as I needed him. In the end, it was Ted who made the decision for me. Family cope after death, but I wasn't sure Ted would. Life goes on and people adapt, but Ted had not been apart from me since he was nine weeks old. He would be devastated without me. Humans understand death and can come to terms with it, but animals can't and often die themselves. I knew that if I died he would be searching for me for the rest of his life. No one would be able to explain to him that I wasn't coming back. I'd seen how distraught Monty was when Penny died, and Ted's heartbreak at losing Monty.

I decided I had to do everything I could to stay alive for his sake. Of course, I worried that if I didn't survive the operation, I would have given Ted even less time with me, but the way things were he was going to live longer than I would. He could have another six years. If I didn't have this operation, I would have to leave him at some point. I kept thinking about the letter Jenny had written to Canine Partners to say that she thought Teddy wouldn't survive without me. I had only one chance and I had to take it.

In the end, I realised I was more afraid of what would happen to Ted than to me. I told my doctor I would have the operation.

The operation was booked for 28 April 2015. I was terrified. I felt like a condemned person. I started to prepare Peter for life without me. I wrote out instructions for how to care for Teddy if I didn't make it through. All his funny ways. The songs I sing when it's time to let his hair down and be silly. I wrote down all his favourite foods and people. Although Teddy officially belonged to Canine Partners, Peter said that he would try to keep him so he didn't have to go to a new home.

All this time, Ted was watching over me, trying to cheer me up, bringing me toys and wagging his tail. He knew I was worried – he just had no idea why.

The morning we were due to go to London, I woke up early and found I'd lost my nerve. I couldn't go through with it. I got dressed to go out on my own to think. Ted wanted to follow me. I sat back on the bed and buried my head in his fur.

I was trapped. If I had the operation and didn't survive, I would leave Ted and Peter. If I didn't have it done, I wouldn't survive for long anyway.

Teddy kept nudging me and licking me: *You all right, Mum? What's wrong?*

I cuddled him and whispered, 'I can't do it, Ted. I'm so sorry, but I can't do this for you.'

It's all going to be all right. I'm here.

'But you don't understand, Teddy, this could kill me. I could die.'

It's all right. You don't have anything to worry about. I'm here.

I hugged him and put my hands in his beautiful golden fur. It was the hardest decision I've ever had to make. In the end, I told Teddy I would go through with it. I had to try it, for him.

We packed the car and left for London. I felt like my world was spinning out of control – all I wanted was for time to stand still. We tried to keep Teddy's routine as normal as possible, so we stopped at all the usual places along our journey. I was having very dark thoughts.

We arrived at St Thomas' in London and had our usual room in the lodge next to the main hospital. I was to stay there for tests prior to my operation, then I would be on the ward.

The first thing we did was take Teddy to the park. We'd got to know several local dogs and their owners who walk in the park every day. I smiled and chatted, but the owners had no idea what was really going on in my head. I wanted to be anywhere but where I was. I wanted to run away.

Teddy sensed I was upset. He wanted cuddling all the time. After my pre-op tests, we took him to Green Park. People stopped and talked to us. Children shook hands with Teddy, and he watched squirrels and ducks. Everything had got very clear, very sharp. Too sharp.

The morning of my operation came and I had never felt so low or so scared. I was woken up by Ted bringing me my slippers. He brought me his lead too: *Come on, let's go for a walk and cheer up.*

I walked round the park in a daze. I could see people talking but couldn't hear what they were saying. I knew this could be the last walk I ever did with Teddy and Peter. I couldn't help thinking about what would happen to them if I didn't make it.

When the time came, I was so worried about Ted being upset that I left him in our hotel room with Peter. When I'd been to theatre before to talk to the surgeon he had come with me, but I thought it would be too distressing this time. I said a cheerful goodbye and told them I wouldn't be long. Ted tried to follow me. Peter offered him treats but he pulled towards me. I shut the door. My stomach did cartwheels. Tears streamed down my face. I could hear Teddy crying for me as I walked to the waiting room to meet my new EB nurse, Annette.

Annette had arranged to meet me in the foyer and walk over to theatre with me. I stood outside the room and thought, *I can't do this. I'll just have to go. I'll walk away and never come back.* Then I thought about how I'd just left Ted and Peter. What on earth would they do without me? I thought about Annette waiting for me. Annette is such a lovely person, you wouldn't do anything to upset her. I went downstairs to meet her. She assured me she would be with me all through the operation and after it, and that Peter and Ted would be waiting in recovery for me.

'I can't do this, Annette,' I said. 'I'm not brave enough. I'm too scared. I'm just not a brave person.'

'Brave people are not the people who aren't scared,' she said. 'Brave people are the ones who are terrified out of their wits and go through with it anyway.'

I still didn't feel brave. Not at all. Even on the operating table, when they were putting equipment on me, I was saying, 'I can't do this.' All I wanted to do was run back to Ted and bury my face in his fur. I worried I hadn't I told Peter or Ted how much I loved them. I went very hot. Unbearably hot and everything floated away.

The next thing I knew I was being licked all over. Every bit of flesh Ted could reach he licked. He whimpered at me and tried to get on the bed. I was in the recovery room and Peter and Ted were there, just as Annette promised. Dear Teddy was beside himself trying to cheer me up.

I had got through it. I'd survived. Ted had saved my life again.

Peter told me later that he and Ted had watched me being wheeled out of theatre. He told me I was trying to open the doors for the surgeons.

'I don't remember that,' I said.

'Well, you never did like sitting still, did you?' he said, smiling. Apparently Ted had been going mad to get at me – Peter had to hold him back.

The pain was out of this world. When I swallowed, it was like swallowing glass. But I'd survived. My daughter Rhiannon and her partner came to see me in the evening. Robert and his wife Samantha were on their way. While they were there, a nurse came into the room and said Ted had to leave.

'I'm sorry,' he said, 'but the dog can't stay with you. Your husband can stay, but the dog will have to go.'

I was horrified.

Rhiannon turned to him. 'Listen,' she said, 'if you take Mum's dog away, I guarantee you've got two seconds before she discharges herself. She will not stay here without Ted. He goes everywhere with her.'

The nurse looked at Rhiannon and then at me and Peter. 'I'll have to ask again,' he said and left the room. He came back a few minutes later and said as long as Ted didn't jump up and bite anyone he could stay. I was very lucky that Rhiannon had been there. Later that night it proved to be the right decision.

My throat felt dreadful. It was swollen and raw. I tried to swallow water but it dribbled out of my mouth. The debris from the dilation was collecting in the bottom of my throat. Every time I tried to sleep the debris made my breathing difficult. It was making a gurgling noise. I tried to cough but it felt I was ripping my throat.

I had let Peter have the bed as there was no way I could sleep. I sat in the chair in the corner. In the early hours of the morning, the debris got stuck and I couldn't breathe. Peter was asleep. I couldn't call out to him and the emergency cord was too far for me to call for help – the drip in my arm was in the way.

I was about to panic when Ted let out a bark. He barked twice and Peter woke up. Peter pressed the button for help and calmed Ted down.

In all my life, I've never felt as secure as I did at that moment. I knew then that Ted would never let me down. He had my life in his paws and there was no one I trusted more.

Epilogue

My Life in His Paws

The operation had been a success. They'd dilated my throat to twelve millimetres. It's still half the size of a normal throat – the webbing is halfway across. My specialist in Exeter was partly right: the muscles were all out of sync when I came round and it took a good month before I could swallow even liquid without feeling I was choking. It took me months to fully recover. I lived on cartons of liquid food from the hospital and even then it was slow going down.

The skin in my oesophagus will never be normal. I still have to liquidise most of my food and it's always painful to swallow and talk. But my throat is so much better than it was before the operation. I just have to hope it stays like this. The doctors have said that it could get worse and they might need to dilate it several more times. I don't know what I'll do if the operation comes round again – I don't think I could face it.

I told Annette, 'Knowing what I know now, I'm not sure I could go through it again. Not even for Ted.'

'We'll have to hope this lasts then,' she said.

But getting through the operation changed me. I became a lot more confident. It sounds funny, but I did. I'd got through my worst fear ever. They said I might not survive it and I did – I can't describe what that feels like. When I walk along, every bird I hear, every tree I see – it's like it's new again. Time is so precious now. Everything is precious.

I feel well now, and everyone says I look well. I just have to take each day as it comes, as I always have.

I hardly ever imagine what life would be like if I didn't have EB. Just occasionally, I let myself wonder what I would do if I had normal skin. And I think, *Gosh, you could do anything. You could go skiing. You could go swimming. You could take up diving. Hockey. Croquet. You could do what you like*. I can't imagine having that freedom. In some ways it's easier having had EB since I was born because I don't know what it's like to live without it. But it doesn't stop you wanting to do things.

Some people say EB gets better as you get older. It's not that the condition gets better – your body is your body, after all. You've got the genetic malfunction and that isn't going to change. But we get better at controlling it. We get better at knowing what we can and can't do. And you can, to a certain extent, limit how much you get hurt. I don't ride horses any more because I know it's not a good idea. If I could, you wouldn't get me off a horse. I'd be living on it, I'd be having my meals on it. I'd be living in my stable with Peter, Ted and my horse. But you learn to adjust.

I haven't given up: I still do things I want to do. But it's always got to be worth it. If I'm going to go out and do the gardening, I know my hands are going to get bad. I know I'm going to get blisters. It's got to be worth it, that drive's got to be there. And I think that as you get older, you get better at working that out. You learn how to balance pain and pleasure. And when I look back, I can see that EB hasn't stopped me doing a lot of things I was told I could never do.

The France plans are still off, but Peter and I are looking for a new home and are hoping to live near a beach in Devon. Teddy loves the beach and the sea. I love seeing him running in and out of the water. He rolls and digs in the sand and seems to laugh at us. He has so many friends to play with. So many people and dogs love him.

Teddy is going to be ten next year. He doesn't act it! He's still so much fun and as cheeky as ever. For his ninth birthday, I took him to the pet shop to buy him a toy. I took two off the shelf and held them up for him.

'Which one would you like for your birthday, Teddy? This one or this one?'

This one! He jumped up and took the one in my right hand, a squeaky caterpillar, with his mouth.

'OK, then,' I said, but before I could put the other one down, he'd jumped up and taken that one too. *And this one, Mum!* Well, then we had to buy them both because they'd been in his mouth. Clever Teddy. He always knows what he's doing.

It's hard to think about, but I know that Teddy's getting to retirement age. Lots of Canine Partners stop work around now and he'll have to retire at twelve, however well he is.

I couldn't bear to lose Teddy, but I don't think I can cope without an assistance dog. When Teddy was ill, I realised just how much he did for me. I don't know what I should do next. If I started training another puppy next year it could be a seamless handover, but I don't want to push Ted's nose out of joint. I think he'd be far more sensitive than Monty. Monty hadn't always been with me, so he could be left with other people. But Teddy and I haven't been separated since he was nine weeks old. And a new puppy would be a lot of work!

If I'm honest, I don't know if I'd survive Ted going, particularly knowing that crying is the worst thing for my throat. Peter has said he doesn't want to be on the planet when I lose Teddy. 'Neither do I,' I said.

I survived losing Monty by having Teddy, so who knows what the future may bring. Teddy might love a puppy to pass on everything he knows to. But hopefully I won't have to make the decision for a while yet. For now I will love and care for Teddy while he loves and cares for me.

Ted is my life. He is my reason to get up in the morning. He keeps me grounded. I know I need to keep looking after him, no matter how bad I feel. He shows me that, however hard things are, life goes on.

With him, I can fly. I don't care what people think of me. If I am OK in his eyes, then I am OK in my eyes – nothing else matters. Every day I think about how lucky I am. I have a faithful, loving, loyal, joyful friend whom I can confidently say has my life in his paws.

I hold his lead, he holds my heart.

epilogue

Just When You Thought
It Was Safe

Over the next few weeks things began to slip back into place. Life was easier. It felt as if a jigsaw had been thrown in the air and the pieces had slowly begun landing in the right places.

The muscles in my throat slowly started to work in harmony making it easier for me to swallow without choking. My confidence was returning. I realised I had made the right decision to have my operation. I couldn't eat any different food than before but what I did eat could go down easier.

At last I felt we could start to plan the summer ahead. We have a motorhome and we were looking forward to visiting family. We had a few practise days out to see how I was coping and all seemed well. I made lists of things to take away and Peter said we could have a holiday in France once I was totally better.

I love the garden and Peter began planting out lots of

bulbs and plants. The greenhouse was full of tomatoes and cucumbers. Ted loved lazing by my feet while I pottered about in the warmth. The apple trees in the orchard were still a mass of blossom. The scent was beautiful. All around the flower beds were seedlings just peeping through the soil. Suddenly life held all sorts of possibilities. I thought of all the adventures we could have. Summer was on its way.

And then disaster struck.

Peter and I were walking Teddy along the Tarka Trail. I took my mobility scooter and Peter walked beside me. Teddy ran along in front of us sniffing every blade of grass.

Life was good. The three of us together in the sunshine.

Teddy's favourite toy is his Frisbee – he loves me to roll it slowly along the ground so that he can run along-side it and pick it up as it rolls. I did this several times and he picked it up and brought it back to me.

He turned to come back and let out the most blood curdling scream. Not a yelp. A scream. It sounded like a human screaming, and then I saw he was standing with his back leg in the air. My first thought was that he had been bitten by a snake. There are adders in the area but I had never seen any along the track. Peter rushed over to Ted who was motionless with his leg still held off the ground. He pushed his head into Peter, he was obviously very distressed.

Peter put his arms under Ted's tummy and supported him, then he lay Ted down and searched his body for a puncture wound. He couldn't find anything. No thorns, no blood. There was no sign of injury. We couldn't work out what had happened to him or why he couldn't put any weight on his left back leg.

We tried to get him onto my scooter but he struggled. We knew he was badly hurt and couldn't risk further injury. Peter said he would run back to the cycle hire to get help.

I stayed with Ted on the floor while Peter ran back Torrington Cycle Hire, where John, the owner sorted out a bike and trailer to get Ted back to the car.

While Peter was gone I rang the vet. He said to get Ted to him as soon as we could.

I phoned canine partners and when I explained Ted's symptoms the lady said she suspected he had probably torn his cruciate ligament. Peter returned with the bike and trailer to transport Ted to the car. It seemed miles. Ted was obviously in a lot of pain. He kept trying to get out of the trailer but I talked to him and told him it was all going to be ok, the vet would make him better. Tears streamed down my face and when Peter turned to talk to me I could see his face was white. We were both so worried. This was our worst moment with Ted.

When we got to the car a friend of ours was there and helped Peter get Ted out of the trailer and into the car. Brian – an ex-marine – easily lifted Ted. I told Brian that it could be a cruciate ligament and he said his dog Poppy had had the same injury a year before and assured me Ted would be fine. Poppy was running about as normal now.

John refused payment for the bike and trailer. He said it was the least he could do and would we let him know how Ted got on at the vet. People are so kind in an emergency.

The journey to the vet seemed forever. I sat in the back of the car to keep Ted still. I had no idea what was going to happen. I rang Canine Partners again on the way. I was so glad I had them to turn to. Sandra, who I spoke to, was calm and explained Ted would need an x-ray and an operation if it was his cruciate ligament. I tried to take in what she was saying but I was in that state of panic where reality and nightmares live. My best boy who is always there for me was hurting and I couldn't ease his pain. I took deep breaths and talked to him until he relaxed into my arms. He gave a very sad sigh and closed his eyes. Slowly, my tears dripped onto his head.

Peter carried Ted into the surgery and he was examined. The vet decided to put him on painkillers for 48 hours and see how he went. If he was no better he would have x-rays to show the damage. The nurse provided us with a belly strap so Peter could support Ted's weight without having to lift him.

We had forgotten about the 12 steep steps on a hillside at the property we were renting. Peter carried Ted into the house but we realised right away we now had a huge problem as we would need to carry Ted up and down the steps each time he needed to see the vet.

The next two days were very upsetting. I could see Teddy was uncomfortable even though he was on painkillers. I slept beside him on the floor and spent every moment with him so that he did not try to follow me anywhere. It was very difficult for him because he had been trained to look after me. Now it was my turn to look after him. I promised him I would stay by his side.

The 48 hours passed but Ted was no better it was obvious that he was still in pain.

We returned to the vet who decided to x-ray him. I had written out a letter to take with him explaining that he would probably be stressed because he is with me 24/7.

I told Ted, as cheerfully as I could, 'Stay there, good boy. I won't be long.' I heard him try to get up to follow me but I just kept going. We went to a café by the river and stayed until it was time to collect him.

People kept arriving at the café with dogs and it only made me miss Ted more. It felt like an eternity before the phone rang to say he could go home. The vet explained that Ted had torn his cruciate ligament and part of his meniscus which would mean an operation called a TTA. It sounded awful. Ted would need bed rest for six weeks and 12 weeks walking on the lead. Ted is always such a happy lively dog, I wasn't sure how he would take being kept still.

I need not have worried. His training really came into its own over the next few weeks. Having been taught not to move until I tell him to he just lay quietly.

With the results confirmed I rang Canine Partners who booked him into St David's vets in Exeter. Mr

Peter Attenburrow has a brilliant reputation for orthopaedic surgery and he was said to be really good with his patients. Human and animals.

The morning of his operation we packed all Ted's medicines and his bed in case he stayed in a long time. Mr Attenburrow had said he would send Ted home as soon as it was safe to do so but we should expect him to stay in overnight. We drove in silence to Exeter apart from saying 'good boy' to Teddy. We had a lovely welcome when we arrived. The nurse, Holly, took Teddy out of the back of the car and showed us in to the practice.

Holly explained what would happen to Ted. We saw Mr Attenburrow who assured us that Ted would be fine.

I couldn't take in what people were saying to me. Ted and I had been together for over seven years. It was a terrible wrench to leave him.

Once again, I had written a long letter explaining all his training cues including things like asking him to toilet and lay quietly etc. Canine Partners have specific cues that all the dogs know. It was better we kept him in the same routine. It would make him feel more secure.

I began to relax when I saw how caring all the staff were. Mr Attenburrow could not have been nicer. He really understood the stress I felt leaving Ted.

We had booked into a hotel in Exeter. There was no way I could go home. I wanted to be able to pick Ted up as soon as we could.

I was beside myself with worry all day. Then the phone rang and Mr Attenburrow said Ted had come round and that the operation had gone really well. Ted would be staying in overnight. I hardly slept.

I was up and ready very early the next morning – like a child at Christmas. The excitement to see Ted again was overwhelming.

When we arrived at the vet's Holly met us and gave us paperwork with all the instructions for rest and feeding. I was on the edge of my seat. I just wanted Ted.

I thought he would try and rush out to me but he was very happy with the nurses. He walked out on his lead. His leg was all shaved and he rested his head against my legs, but he was very quiet. Not like Ted at all.

Holly put him in the car. I bent forward to kiss him and he put his head under my hair and leant against my neck, just like when I first met him.

You can't cry. It's not fair on the animals. It distresses them. But it was so hard not to. Partly because his leg looked so hurt and partly with relief to hold him again.

Ted was to have bed rest for a month at least. I thought that would be impossible.

When we got home I asked Peter to help me onto the floor so I could lie close to Ted. We slept like this all afternoon. Now the worry and fear had left my body I was totally exhausted.

Peter said he came into the room to check we were both ok and Ted had reached out and put his paw on my arm.

When I awoke two big brown eyes were watching

me. He slowly wagged his tail. I kissed the paw he had put on my arm and stroked his beautiful head.

Ted managed to eat a soft food diet and Peter helped him out to the toilet.

That night I kept waking and watching to see he was still breathing as he had not moved a muscle. When I bent down to stroke him he gently licked my hand.

Jane, Toby's mum came to see him the second day without Toby. Usually Ted would go to meet her at the door and take her scarf from her to bring to me. This time he just lay there. It took us both all our strength not to cry. This wasn't the Ted we knew. He managed to give a few slow thumps of his tail but otherwise he didn't move.

Over the next few weeks I didn't leave Ted at all. Only to go to the bathroom. He was so used to following me; I couldn't risk him standing on his poorly leg..

Peter had to go back to staying awake while I slept. One of us needed to be aware of my breathing.

It really hit home how much we depended on Ted to watch me.

I was riddled with guilt that I had caused him all this pain by rolling his Frisbee, but the vet assured me the cruciate could have gone at any time.

One day I got out the book that I had started to write years before. My days were spent writing more of the book, and in between massaging Teddy and looking after him.

Peter Attenburrow told us not to travel with Ted in the car any more than was vital as it would hurt his leg.

We didn't mind. This was Ted's time; this was what a true partnership was all about.

My family and friends rang for regular updates. We didn't allow any visitors during the first six weeks apart from Jane. He would probably get too excited and we wanted him to have the best possible chance of a full recovery. After 14 days he had his stitches out and the wound had healed really nicely. We took Ted back to Exeter after a month for a check up. Mr Attenburrow was really pleased with his progress. He said that after eight weeks post-op he would advise us about physio and hydrotherapy. We were now able to start walking him very carefully, strictly timing everything. We started with 20 seconds twice a day. After a few days we were adding up to 30 seconds until he managed two ten minute walks. It was looking good. I was constantly in contact with Canine Partners for updates and advice. I was so glad of their support. I would not have wanted to go through this alone. The forced rest was allowing time for my mind and body to heal.

At six weeks post-op our local vet said to try Ted on the treadmill to help his muscles. He had two sessions that week but he went really lame. It had not suited him. We mde an appointment to see Peter Attenburrow in Exeter to see why Ted was so lame. I was devastated. My world spun out of control and I tried not to cry. My heart was breaking.

We came home with more painkillers and steroids and antacids to help prevent damage to his insides from the steroids. Just like me.

No one can imagine how low I felt. He was to rest for another 2 weeks and start trying to walk again from scratch. Apart from his vet visits I had not left the house at all in six weeks.

I found it so painful to watch something I thought was entirely my fault. A good friend knew I was very depressed and she suggested I should go out for an hour a day otherwise I would be really ill. I only managed half an hour the first day as I knew Teddy would miss me greatly and I didn't want him to try and stand up to follow me.

It was very difficult to get used to being with a human carer again and not with Ted. I was very grateful for the help but it just wasn't Ted.

Looking back, I realise those times out saved my sanity. I couldn't go on with the guilt and just sit there watching him. I think I could cope with it when I was helping but when I felt I had allowed him more pain it was more than I could cope with.

Teddy was always so pleased to see me when I came home. You would think I had been gone a year.

Each day I began to write more and more. One day when I had taken Teddy out for his five 5 minute walk in the garden the phone rang. It was my agent. For a moment I didn't recognise his voice. Jon had rung to say that he wanted to go ahead with my book. Hodder & Stoughton wanted to publish it. I was so excited I couldn't take in what he was saying. It turned out to be just what I needed. I threw myself into writing every day.I love a challenge, I made a plan to walk Ted and write. After all, I had plenty of time on my hands. The weather had become too hot for Teddy to go outside anyway. In hot weather we only take him out early morning and late evening as the tarmac can get very hot for his paws.

Once Teddy was able to walk for ten minutes a day again we asked if it was okay for him to start hydro-therapy – swimming rather than a treadmill. We were recommended to take him to Okehampton to The Retreat, run by Duncan. I must admit I was really unsure about him doing anything in water after the experience on the treadmill. When I contacted Duncan he assured me that there would be two people in the water at all times with Teddy, and that they would take great care of him.

When Teddy saw the swimming pool he couldn't get in fast enough. They put a life jacket on him even though they were going to hold onto him. He loved it. Duncan, Alex and Irene gave Teddy just a few minutes on the first day. The next day Teddy seemed much more mobile. We started to take him twice a week and we never looked back. It was wonderful to see him swim-ming. He was able to play in the water where he couldn't on land. He swam after the ball and thoroughly enjoyed himself. Duncan and the team were brilliant. After Teddy's swimming he was taken into a shower room where he was washed and shampooed, and then into the drying room. It is such a well thought-out building. My confidence began to return. I could begin to see that Teddy would be walking properly and running about again in the near future.

A few months later we returned to see Peter Attenburrow. He said Teddy had built up some really good muscles and that it must've been the swimming that had achieved so much in such a short time. He gave Teddy the all-clear and said he didn't need to see him again, but if we had any concerns at all we were welcome to contact him. I was over the moon and rang Canine Partners to tell them the news – they were thrilled. They never doubted for one moment that Ted would get well.

It wasn't all doom and gloom as Teddy was recovering. I tried to think of things he could do without having to get up. I remembered seeing DHK teaching the dogs to read and thought this was a great idea. I wrote the word 'sleep' on a piece of card and held it up. I told Teddy to sleep and the minute he put his head on his paws I clicked and gave him a treat. After a few tries of this he was soon sleeping every time I held the card up. I couldn't believe he had learned so quickly.

I also put several items within nose touching reach for him and taught him lots more names for them. He loved it. He was such an active dog, I realised how hard it was for him to stay still for this length of time. Ted could not have been a better patient. I was glad he knew his cues, once told to go to bed he never gets out until he is asked to. This was very valuable during his bed rest.

One day, not long ago I took him shopping. He picked the bread up for me and took it to the checkout.

He couldn't manage to put it up on the counter. He sat back, thought about it and turned his head. Then he threw it as he turned back to face the checkout lady. It sailed through the air. I had a sudden vision of it hitting the bottles of wine on the shelves behind the counter. Whenever we see the lady she calls out, 'that's the dog that throws the bread at me!' and we both laugh.

One of my proudest moments was to take Ted to London to meet the team at Hodder & Stoughton. Ted even went to the groomers the day before. I was so nervous but I need not have worried. Everyone was so friendly. I was very excited, all I could think was how special Ted was, how he had saved my life and given me the confidence to write. I was up floating in the ceiling.

We discussed plans and decided to launch the book with Canine Partners at Crufts the following March. I would be asked to attend book signings and talks. It was like a dream.

While we were at Crufts several people gave Ted treats to take home. He had been chatting to a lady dog on Facebook called Baby Hope and her mum delivered treats and a toy from her. Yes I kid you not, other dogs do write to Ted.

A lovely lady came to see me and she gave me a silver paw print on a chain. To this day I wear it every day. If she reads this, thank you – it is very special to me.

Ted has lots of social media accounts including Instagram, Twitter and Facebook where we interact with people who have read the book – I love hearing how much people enjoy hearing about Ted. I just wish Ted knew what joy he brings to everyone he meets. I always say he has a sense of humour. He loves to carry an umbrella. I knew he was feeling better after his operation when I started walking him outside the garden and he was carrying an umbrella which he banged along some railings, making a tune. He is such a character.

People write to me or stop me on the street and say they had never heard of EB before they read my book. They also say they are amazed at what Ted can do. That is brilliant news to me. I wanted to write to raise awareness of both charities.

I do not think we as humans have scratched the surface of what dogs are capable of. With kindness and patience they can be taught to respond to so many cues. If they are physically able to do a task then I see no reason they cannot be taught it.

My sister, Mary, was in a hospice while Ted was recovering, so as soon as he got the all-clear we set off in our motorhome to see her.

We had previously visited Mary and as soon as we got there Ted took me to where he thought the room was but they had moved Mary to another room. Poor Ted was so surprised when he couldn't find her. He never forgets a route or a place he has been. We often say he would've made a very good guide dog.

We went into Mary's room and Teddy was so pleased to see her, he is not a licky dog but he gave Mary is really good wash. I realised then that she was not well at all.

The hospice is in a beautiful setting surrounded by fields and trees. Mary had a bird feeder on her room window which fascinated Teddy. We watched the birds fly in and out – the look on his face was a picture. We sat talking with Mary for a little while then took Teddy out into the grounds so that Mary could rest and he could roll and play. One day when he had been out playing and performing a lady approached me and asked if you could visit her brother who was quite poorly.

I said to her, 'What a shame you missed Teddy doing his training'.

She laughed and said,'I didn't miss him at all I was videoing him out of the upstairs window!' We both laughed. It turned out that all the visitors and staff were being entertained by Ted. I explained that Teddy is a PAT dog as well as a Canine Partner and that we would be honoured to see her brother.

We took Teddy into a room where we were introduced to a man named Tony.

Tony asked if Ted could get on the bed beside him. I explained that Ted doesn't get on beds at all. He prefers his own bed to mine. He only gets on our bed if I am very ill. Then Teddy did something he never ever does, he slowly climbed onto the bed beside Tony. I was so surprised. I went to stop him but the family said that Tony would love to be able to cuddle Teddy.

When Teddy got on the bed beside Tony he put his

head over Tony's body and his paws over his legs. He had never done this before – not even for me. He stayed like that for quite a while. We all talked about the things Ted helps me with and Tony told us about his work as a paramedic. He was such a lovely man. I always think that animals are a good judge of character. I will never forget Ted lying beside Tony. I knew Ted had a beautiful heart and that it was capable of loving others as well as me. My greatest joy is sharing Ted.

I spent precious moments with Mary. We laughed and talked, sharing happy memories. Mary rallied and was able to go home. She knew I was planning to go to France when she was better and she insisted we should go.

On the ferry I felt uneasy. Mary seemed so much better but alarm bells kept ringing.

After only a few days I received a phone call to say Mary was very poorly and was in hospital. I couldn't think straight. My stomach was in such a tight knot I felt sick.

We took Ted to the vet for his worming tablet that he has to have 24 hours before sailing back to the U.K. That 24 hours seemed like a lifetime.

I had nursed my mother 35 years earlier with cancer and she had died in my arms. History was repeating itself and I had no control to stop it. I began having nightmares. I would be woken by Ted nudging my arm and making whining noises.

The hour-and-a-half on the boat seemed like

eternity. I watched as the white cliffs appeared and part of me wanted to run away.

When we arrived at the hospital it was a lovely evening but it felt so wrong. I was in a very dark place. I knew my time with my beautiful sister was nearing the end.

Over the next few days we popped in for a few minutes each evening. These moments were so precious. I wanted to store each second in my memory for all eternity. Mary became weaker but she looked so beautiful. She still smiled and chatted but she was sleeping a lot more. On one visit I just sat with her while she slept. Then I knew it was time to say goodbye. I needed to leave her and let her family have their time with her.

For the first time ever I didn't take Ted to see her. Mary asked where he was and I said it was too hot to take him into the hospital. I had to leave him with Peter. Ted had sensed my distress on the journey and I knew I would really upset him if I cried. It's no use telling me not to cry when my heart is torn apart.

Mary was asleep when I got there. It wasn't visiting time but the nurse said it was okay to see her as I explained I was going home.

After a while Mary woke and asked for water. It was to be the last thing I did for her.

She smiled and I told her I was going home. I would see her soon. We both knew I wouldn't. I hugged her and said, 'be good'.

'I'll try,' she said and I walked away smiling until I got out of the door. Then the tears streamed down my face. I tried to sing a tune Mary used to dance to but all I heard were sobs.

When I got home Ted was beside himself. He licked every available piece of flesh he could find. He licked away my tears and I put my face in his fur and cried.

Mary was moved to the hospice where she sadly died two days later.

With no black allowed at the funeral it was a beautiful service. Her girls Tracy and Juliette read a letter to mum. I was so proud of them. Her wicker casket was covered in flowers. There was standing room only in the church. All her school and work friends were there. Mary loved to dance and her line-dance and tea-dance friends were there too. You could see how loved Mary was.

During the quiet time in the service tears ran down my face and Ted, who had been lying quietly, got up and pushed against my legs. He was grinning and he only does this when I am really upset.

I fought back the tears and assured him I was ok. He wasn't convinced but he lay down again and stared up at me.

I had lost my sister, my best friend and my anchor. Life would never be the same.

During the last two years I had been through the three worse times in my life. Peter and Ted had steered me through the stormy waters.

Not being able to cry is the worse part of EB. Crying had affected my throat and even as I write my swallowing is not as good as it was. Without Ted I know I would cry rivers. Knowing how upset he gets is the only thing that stops me completely wrecking my throat.

Ted has completely recovered from his operation. As I write this he is lying by my side. His friend Toby is staying here on his holiday while Jane is in Spain. They have just been playing on our local beach. He is running about as normal. You would never know he had had an injury. He doesn't act nine.

He runs about and every now and again he turns to me and says, 'You ok mum?'

'Yes I'm fine Ted, after all, I hold your lead – you hold my heart.'

Help and Resources

These are some of the organisations that have helped me over the years and may be of help to others:

Canine Hydrotheraphy without the help of Duncan and his team Ted would never have recovered as quickly as he did.
www.caninehydrotheraphy.co.uk

Canine Partners for providing Ted, all their help, and having faith in us. I hope we made you proud.
www.caninepartners.co.uk

Clicker training, a wonderful way of training dogs. For more information, this is a useful site: www.clickertraining.com

DEBRA for providing nurses and social care. Having help from this charity made living with EB a lot easier. It provides valuable nursing staff who are always on hand to help us.
www.debra.org.uk

Livescribe is an amazing smart pen that enabled me to handwrite text, that it then downloaded to my computer and converted it into typescript. Thank you, Ruth, for finding this for me.
www.livescribe.com

Magloc, who make magnetic lead connectors for Ted's harness. They are so much easier to use than clips. Great for sore hands as well as using in wet weather.
www.magloc.co.uk

Peter Attenburrow is an Advanced Practitioner in Small Animal Orthopaeedics. I will always be grateful to Peter for not only mending Ted but his kindness to us all during such a difficult time. He always believed Ted would run on the beach again, and he does.

Pets As Therapy provides therapeutic visits to hospitals and a variety of other venues by volunteers with their own friendly dogs and cats.
www.petsastherapy.org

Puffing Billy, where the book was started and finished. They must have thought I'd moved into the cafe. Thank you for the hot fires and coffee.
www.puffingbilly.com

Remap, a voluntary charity of retired engineers who help solve problems for disabled people. They made me a connector to attach Ted's trailer to my scooter.
www.remap.org.uk

The Sohana Research Fund is a charity dedicated to funding research and clinical trials into the treatment of EB. www.sohanaresearchfund.org

Ted's web page has links to his Facebook page and to YouTube, where you can see more of Ted's training videos. www.mylifeinhispaws.co.uk

Acknowledgements

To Jon, Kate, Nicola, Fiona, Charlotte, Jenni and Naomi – without all your help this book would not be here today. I'm thrilled to be part of Hodder & Stoughton.

Do you wish this wasn't the end?

Join us at www.hodder.co.uk, or follow us on
Twitter @hodderbooks to be a part of our community
of people who love the very best in books and reading.

Whether you want to discover more about a book
or an author, watch trailers and interviews, have the
chance to win early limited editions, or simply browse
our expert readers' selection of the very best books,
we think you'll find what you're looking for.

And if you don't,
that's the place to tell us what's missing.

We love what we do, and we'd love you to be part of it.

www.hodder.co.uk

@hodderbooks

HodderBooks

HodderBooks